YouTube Mastery

How to get 10,000 views per month, explode your traffic and grow your business with YouTube

First Edition

May 2016

By Tim Levy

Title: *10,000 Views on YouTube*

Subtitle: *How to get to 10,000 views a month on YouTube*

Author: *Tim Levy*

Published by: *Tim Levy and Associates*

First Edition, May 2016

Published in the United States of America

Dedication

This book is dedicated to my amazing team including

- my lovely wife Angela,
- our (mostly) angelic children, Zak, Finn and Bella
- my parents Anita and Chris
- my incredible support team including Andrea, Sally, Angela, Dan, Pablo and Joel in particular

… and the 1,000 (and more) people we're hoping to help with books just like this.

Contents

Introduction 11

    Important Questions.. 11

        Who Am I and Why Should You Listen to Me? 12

        Who Is This Book For? 13

        What will you discover in this book?....................... 15

        How hard is this? 16

Section One / Key Concepts 21

    Key Concept #1 – What is traffic (and why do we care)? 21

    The 3-Axis Model 21

    The Four Traffic Ecosystems 26

        1 - Search Traffic 26

        2 - Social Media Traffic 28

        3 - Purchase Traffic....................................... 29

        4 - Video Traffic 30

Key Concept #2 – What is SEO?..33

    An SEO Example 34

    What is YouTube SEO? 38

    Setting Expectations 38

    The Google Bonus..40

    How does YouTube SEO actually work? 43

    The Iron Filings SEO Analogy 44

Section Two / Video Tips and Structure...................................51

Video Production Tips..52

    Tip #1 - The Basics..52

    Tip #2 – Lights, Camera and Sound...................53

    Tip #3 – Our Equipment List.............................55

    Tip #4 - Location 56

Video Structure 57

    Why Is Structure So Important? 57

The Four Critical Pieces 59

    A Quick Example 59

    Section One – The Introduction 66

    Section Two – The Logo 69

    Section Three – Content with Bug 70

    Section Four - Call-to-action 72

Recap 75

Doing the Magic 76

    Fiverr.com 76

    Videohive.Com 83

Section Three / Getting Ready to Post 89

Step 1 – Hunting for Keywords 91

Step 2 - Transcript of the Video 99

Step 3 – Designing a Thumbnail 105

    Thumbnails from Fiverr 107

    Thumbnails from Graphic River 109

Step 4 – Optimizing Filenames.................................110

Recap with another Example 113

    Firstly – we must Hunt for Keywords. 114

    Secondly – Get a transcript.................................118

    Thirdly – Get a Thumbnail 118

    Finally, Optimize Filenames.................................119

Section Four / Posting the Video 124

Step 1 - Uploading 124

Step 2 - Filling in the Fields.................................129

    Title Field 129

    Tags 129

    Description.................................130

    Adding a Bio 132

Steps 3 - Publishing the Video 135

Step 4 - Closed Captions 136

    Setting the Timings 139

Section Five / Measuring the Results 146

Tracking the 123RF Video 146

Tracking the VideoHive video 153

Troubleshooting: Fixing or Changing a Keyword 154

Section Six / Wrapping It All Up 162

The 10,000 Views 163

The Wild West 165

YouTube Mastery

Introduction

JOEL FOUND IT DIFFICULT
TO SEPARATE REAL
FROM VIRTUAL TRAFFIC.

Introduction

Welcome to YouTube Mastery 101, the book designed to get you everything you could possibly want from your YouTube experience.

What do we want?

- We want lots of videos to rank lots of keywords to generate lots of views every month.
- We want videos to generate clicks and direct people to your business, your website or wherever you wish your audience to go.

And we want it to happen fast! **It's all about the traffic** and YouTube is sensational for just that purpose.

Important Questions

Let's talk about YouTube Mastery 101. You probably have some important questions right now like –

- Who is this guy and why should I listen to him?
- Who is this book for, anyway?
- What can I hope to discover in this book?

- How hard is this? Can I even do it?

So, let's get right to it!

YouTube Mastery 101 is about getting your video structured right, then up and online with optimal SEO for YouTube. It's about getting your videos discovered, clicked on and driving traffic to your business or project in a simple, repeatable way that pretty much anyone can do.

It's about structuring, preparing and then posting your video as effectively as possible for the highest possible rank. Done correctly, it's possible to rank YouTube videos in minutes where you might struggle for months with normal Google SEO and still get almost nowhere!

Who Am I and Why Should You Listen to Me?

My name is Tim Levy. I run a digital strategy and production agency out of Austin, Texas. I'm also a professional speaker, coach, consultant, author and entrepreneur. You might have seen me around on radio or television or you might have seen some of my books.

My other books include –

- **The Google Gamble** which is all about search traffic on Google.
- **The Entrepreneurial Handbook** which is all about building virtual teams for almost nothing.
- **The Fast Book Handbook** which is about how to get a book up and for sale in as few as ten working hours.
- **Creativity and Innovation** which is about getting into the optimum state for creativity and staying there.
- **The Awakener's Handbook** which is about being fully awake and bringing others along with you.
- **The Life Summit** which is about assessing and optimizing your life now and for the future.

There are other books as well, but that's probably enough for now. You can cruise my web site at www.timlevy.net if you'd like to know more.

Who Is This Book For?

This book is for anyone who wants to generate traffic online, then convert those prospects to a specific action for their business, project or purpose. This book is for people who want to better understand how to manage online traffic. For traffic to become meaningful for a business or mission, we must understand how traffic works and how best to monetize it.

Video is, simply put, far more engaging and compelling than any written copy. And what's more, YouTube itself is growing exponentially. It already has over 1.5 billion users viewing over 3 billion videos on the site *every day*. And the number of hours/month people spend on YouTube has been growing every year.

And what are they looking for? Everything. YouTube is the number two search engine in the world with more traffic than the next twelve combined.

Why am I telling you this? I'm telling you this because it means that if you're not on YouTube, you should be. If you're not on YouTube, you're missing out on the largest slice of available traffic online right now and I'm including Google in that statement. Getting solid search results on Google can be a never-ending gamble. While we can attempt to wrangle Google's algorithm, we will never quite fully understand it! But meanwhile, we can rank a video on YouTube in a matter of minutes.

What this means is that this book is for everyone who would like to drive people to a web site, business or project. This book is for anyone who would like to grow their business in the most engaging way possible, by using video!

Of course, right now I'm assuming you can turn on a PC, maintain basic computer skills and produce a video. This is *not* a book about cameras and editing and video production. I'm assuming you have a free YouTube account as well as an internet connection. We will need both to upload and SEO your videos.

Other than that, this book will tell you everything you need to know. Seem fair?

What will you discover in this book?

Here's a quick overview of the book's overall structure.

1. In Section One, we'll introduce **the key concepts**
2. In Section Two, we'll look at an **optimal video structure** for YouTube videos that gets the most out of the platform

3. In Section Three, we'll look at the **YouTube SEO preparation** you should do *before* you post on YouTube

4. In Section Four, we'll get to where the rubber really meets the road as we go through our **specific posting sequence**

5. In Section Five, having posted your video, it's important to measure the result. Otherwise how do you know if your video is performing as you wish? We go through the process of **tracking rankings**.

6. Finally, in Section Six we bring everything together and wrap it all up, and talk about some **next steps** you might want to take.

How hard is this?

Seriously, how hard is this? We've all been promised "easy results" and then discovered it's just too hard to follow directions. The instructor uses terms you've never heard of, or shows you a single easy way to do something, then expects you to be able to do the difficult next step alone. I won't do that. We're going to work this through methodically with screenshots along the way.

Let me set some expectations. I've had quite a few beta-testers working on this book. They all report that, having read through the steps in the book (or watched it as the online course available on Udemy via at www.timlevy.net/youtube) they can post their first video in a matter of hours. Then, with a few repetitions and practice, they can post a video going through this entire process in an hour (or less). And honestly, a little practice will make it even quicker; the people on my crew report achieving the entire posting process in fifteen minutes or less.

You can get there too.

If you need to ask anything, you can talk to me! I love answering questions so feel free to reach out at any time. Jump to www.timlevy.net/contact and just email me. It is my intention to make this as effective and complete a guide for you as possible.

So, let's jump right into Section One and the first key concept.

Section One

Key Concepts

HOW AM I SUPPOSED TO KNOW
WHAT YOUR KEYWORD IS?

Section One / Key Concepts

Key Concept #1 – What is traffic (and why do we care)?

The first key concept is **traffic**. What do I mean by that? And why do I keep talking about it as if it's really important?

Well, let me explain.

Firstly, let's be clear. I definitely don't mean the sort of traffic where you get stuck on a freeway. I mean **online traffic** or **website traffic**.

Before we start, however, I should really go back a step or two and introduce the 3 Axis model.

The 3-Axis Model

The **Three Axis Model** is something I've developed over time as a simple model that describes every business. It has been helpful to hundreds of CEOs and entrepreneurs over the decade. In other words, every business has and needs these three axes. Let's have a look.

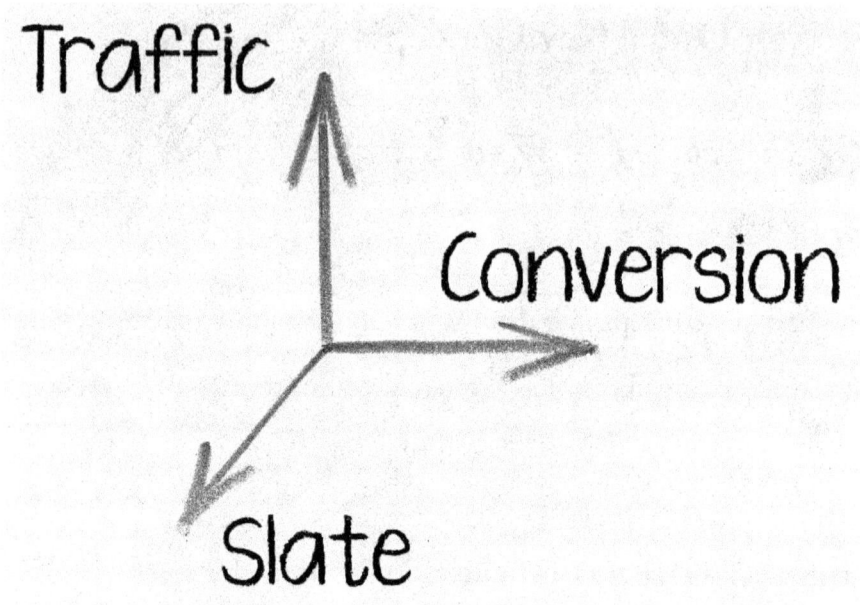

Here we have the three critical axes for any business.

1. The first axis is **traffic**.

2. The second axis is **conversion**.

3. The third axis is **slate**.

Generating Traffic is all about bringing new people and new business to your door. It is mission critical for every business from manufacturing to construction. It's mission critical for Business to Business and Business to Consumer businesses. It's mission critical to every business whether you're promoting a book, selling an album, educating people or just mucking around with your new kids' blog. It's what separates success from failure whether you're selling some random widget on Amazon, providing a service to other businesses or trying to bring people to your physical shopfront. Traffic is everything!

Or is it? While traffic is the critical life blood for almost[1] every business, traffic *without* conversion is useless. So, what is the second axis all about?

Conversion is taking someone from *"I'm interested"* to *"I'm in!"* Conversion is about taking someone from bring a *potential* to an *actual* client. And so conversion, our second axis, is also mission critical to every business.

Of course, there are different levels of conversion. Here are a few examples of behavior your audience can partake in, signifying "conversion" has occurred.

- signing up for a newsletter
- liking a video
- subscribing to a channel

---

[1] OK – so I can think of a few exceptions. For example, if you have a permanent government contract or a research grant. Are there any other exceptions you can think of? Let me know!

- picking up the phone and calling you
- actually buying something!

One way or another, you're going to need all of these things. **Conversion** is critical and without it all the traffic in the world means nothing. So, what is the last axis?

Slate, the third axis, refers to a list of products and services that vary in price and delivery over time. It's like the old slate a grocer would use to list all the items he had for sale. In other words, you have things that are cheap and things that are expensive, and you have things that are one-shot deals bought once (like a book) and things that are bought over a long period (like a master-class or a year's subscription to cable TV).

When you have **all three axes in a healthy state you have a healthy business**. Mostly, however, when I run into CEOs and entrepreneurs, they have unhealthy axes and therefore, unhealthy businesses. And what happens when you have a weakness in even just one axis? You go the way of the dinosaurs, my friend.

"YOUTUBE IS BASICALLY TWITTER
FOR PEOPLE WHO
CAN'T BE BOTHERED TO READ
140 CHARACTERS"

The Four Traffic Ecosystems

So, what do you need to know about traffic? Firstly, there are four critical traffic ecosystems.

What are they?

1. The first is **search** traffic.
2. The second is **social media** traffic.
3. The third is **purchase** traffic.
4. The fourth is **video** traffic.

1 - Search Traffic

The first traffic ecosystem is **search traffic**. If you have ever used Google or read about Google, then you understand that significance of page rank. If you're an internet nerd (like me) you might have heard about something called search engine optimization (**SEO**). Understanding SEO is imperative to a high web rank, but it's not just related to Google.

When your Google SEO is good, people find you when they search for things on Google. When your Google SEO is bad no one's finding you, so you get no traffic. Simple, right?

Luckily, there's an entire industry that has popped up to help you with your web site's Google SEO. Having said that, Google has not published the details of their algorithm and I imagine they never will. That makes it an increasingly complex guessing game as I've laid out in my book *The Google Gamble*. And even when you get it right, it can take months and more to get a trackable and helpful result.

Unluckily, the Google SEO industry (those consultants and geeks who claim they will fix your SEO forever) has proven to be full of what I would term *snake oil salesmen*. Of course, I have only anecdotal experience generated as I speak to audiences of CEOs across the country. A large proportion of them relate bad SEO experiences as they're taken advantage of again and again. In a recent call, less than a month ago, I was referred to someone who had spent $25,000 on SEO without any measurable results. I know because I googled the company and came up with zilch!

So, Google SEO can be tricky. What other options are there to generate traffic?

2 - Social Media Traffic

The second critical ecosystem for traffic is social media. It is possible to generate amazing traffic through web sites like Facebook, Instagram, Twitter and the other big social media web sites. Facebook alone has more than 1.5 billion members. That's just one web site!

Having said that, there is old school social media and new school social media. The old-school method of social media is to simply post a whole lot of content on Facebook and hope for the best. Companies used to "hope" a relevant audience would find their words and images, wind up at their web site and convert into actual customers. If you catch my drift, the old-school method doesn't really work all that well. You can't just sit passively back and hope for the best. You must understand the mechanics of the machine you're working with to produce results. The saddest part of this story is that many social media professionals *still work this way!*

The new school social media methods, based on proven and guaranteed results are the way to go. This book is about YouTube;

you'll need my Small Business / Massive Growth book to find out how to rock social media in this way.

3 - Purchase Traffic

The next ecosystem is **purchase**; in other words, the web sites where people are **buying things online**. The next space we'd like to observe are websites where people can actively purchase items online. So where are people buying things online? Of course, we're talking about www.amazon.com. This one web site is currently generating $178 billion p.a. in net revenue (per www.statista.com). That's more than the next dozen retailers' revenue combined, and that includes Wal-Mart and Apple! Some estimate Amazon's market share of all online sales to be as high as 70% (although that sounds high to me). The moral of the story is, if you're not on Amazon, then you're not really selling online, are you?

For people selling *things*, being active in the purchasing ecosystem is super important.

There's a whole world of Amazon SEO for you to discover which must be a cue for yet another book, right? So where does that leave us? I left the best traffic ecosystem to last – **video.**

4 - Video Traffic

The fourth and final ecosystem is **video traffic.** It is here that we are experiencing explosive growth. Let's have a quick look at the annual numbers here (current in 2017;

- Number of people using YouTube – 1.5 billion
- YouTube's estimated annual revenue - $10 billion
- Video hours watched per month – 6 billion
- Average time spent on YouTube per session – 40 minutes
- Percentage of millennials that use YouTube – 81%

These stats come from a company called DMR which focuses on digital marketing stats (www.expandedramblings.com). They illustrate how YouTube has turned from a little side project for Google to an industry mover and shaker, practically overnight.

And that's why it's such a good time to get started on YouTube – before everyone else finds out about it! In time, it may become as crowded and untenable as Google is right now.

That's what traffic is; we've answered our first key question and explained our first key concept. In summary, traffic is people showing up at your business. It's important **because every business needs people to buy their products and services**. It makes fundamental sense, right?!

"FOR THE LAST TIME IT'S
S FOR SUPER –
NOT S FOR SEO"

Key Concept #2 – What is SEO?

This is a book about mastering YouTube SEO for the purpose of ranking your videos and driving traffic to your web site. But what does SEO even mean? It's an acronym that stands for **Search Engine Optimization**.

OK – so what does *that* mean?!

Simply put, **Search Engine Optimization is the art and science of being found.** Google SEO is the art and science of *being found on Google*. Amazon SEO is the art and science of being found on Amazon. YouTube SEO, therefore, is the art and science of *being found on YouTube*.

When someone types an enquiry on a search engine such as Google, YouTube or Amazon or anywhere else, a load of responses come up. You want your business to be at the very top where possible, right? That means you'll need to understand how the algorithm works that creates those ranking decisions.

An SEO Example

So, what does that look like in the real world? Here's a screenshot of YouTube.com as it stands today.

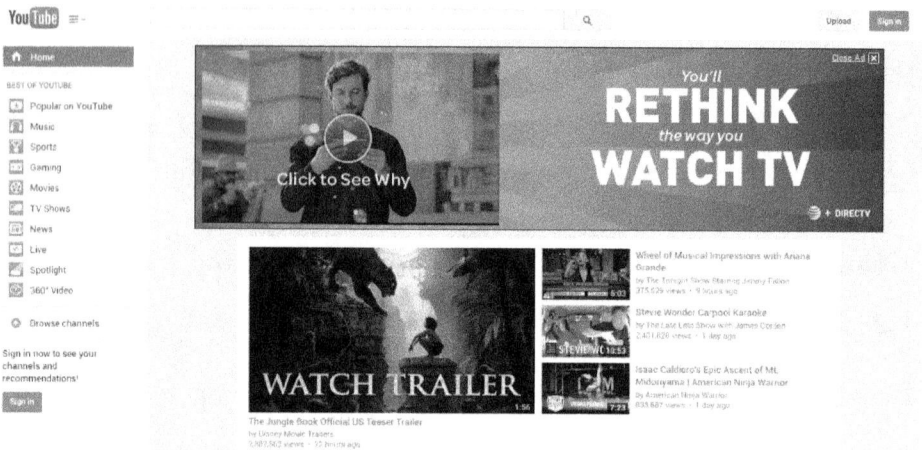

Of course, your screen will look slightly different since it changes a little bit every day. However, the key building blocks, however, will be the same. We have –

- The navigation on the left
- The search box up top
- Upload and login buttons top right
- An ad front and center – in this case for DirecTV
- Various recommended videos, channels and playlists below

Interestingly, YouTube will base these recommendations and ads on your viewing history. If you watch lots of music videos, you'll see lots of music videos recommended. If you watch lots of gaming, you'll see gaming videos, channels and ads. In this case, since I'm not logged in, it has no idea of who I am and gives me fairly random advice.

Now, let's see what happens when we search for something. In this case, I'm going to type in 'Elance Tutorial' and this is what pops up.

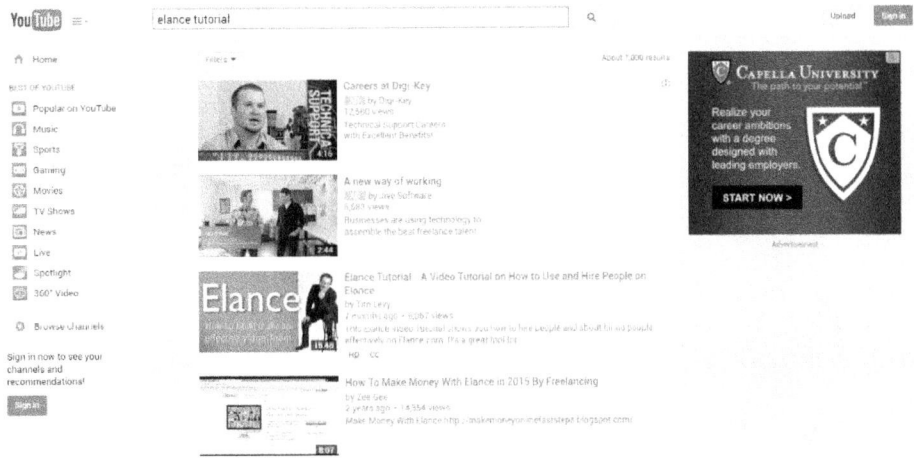

OK – so certain things stay the same.

- The navigation is still on the left
- The upload and sign in buttons are still top right

- The huge ad for "Direct TV" has vanished and has been replaced by what YouTube thinks is a relevant ad on the right, in this case for Capella University where presumably you learn how to sing without accompaniment. OK – relax - just a little college humor there, my friends.
- Most importantly, the search bar now has 'Elance tutorial,' where I typed it in.

Underneath, however, things have really changed. We have a wealth of search results. YouTube has run its search engine optimization algorithm and decided that the four videos you see are the top results. The top two, you'll notice, have a little 'AD' box next to them. That shows that these are not organic search results but instead, the results of paid advertising.

The first organic result is a video with a little picture of yours truly sitting on a stool. We consider that to be the first ranking in the organic search results, so we say that this video is ranked #1 for the keyword search term 'Elance tutorial'. And that's good. It means that this video will get lots of people looking at it every month. In this case, the video has received as many as 1,000 views every 30 days as this little graph shows.

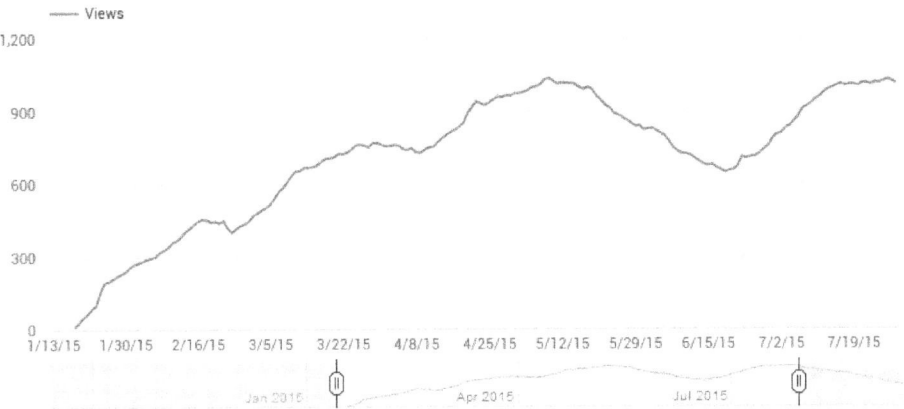

OK, this graph is a little technical. I admit that! Let me explain.

Firstly – where does it come from? It's a screenshot from YouTube analytics, which is a free service included with your YouTube account. It allows you to track your results, make good decisions and influence the fate of each video. That's good, right?

Secondly – what does it mean? In this case, it's showing the number of views this video has enjoyed over 30 days. You can see it started at 0 views when it started around 1/13/15. It has wiggled and moved as we tweaked the SEO until it hit more than 1,000 views a month around 5/12/15. At that point, something changed on YouTube and it moved gently down. We re-optimized the video listing and it went back up – and so it goes.

Do you get the idea? YouTube SEO is the art and science of making the curve go *up*. And up is good!

What is YouTube SEO?

As we've said and now shown, SEO is all about *being found*. YouTube SEO, therefore, is about being found on YouTube.

Most people don't really consider YouTube to be an SEO engine. They don't understand it has an SEO algorithm written behind it, but it really does. When you master the YouTube algorithm and therefore YouTube SEO your YouTube videos will vastly improve their odds of being found. Some YouTube videos randomly find their own traffic but most don't; they need some extra love in the form of the YouTube SEO we're about to lay out now.

Setting Expectations

What results can you hope or even expect to get?

I have found over time that when you have made great content (and I'll talk more about that soon), you can expect to be found hundreds of times a month. Some videos will be found thousands of times a month, if you are really terrific. Our top videos get over 3,000 views per month purely with organic search traffic. While that will not happen *all* the time, you can expect maybe hundreds and eventually thousands of views for your videos as you get better and better at this process.

Let's do the math.

- If you have 100 videos getting 100 views, that's 10,000 views a month
- If you have 10 videos getting 1000 views, that's also 10,000 views a month
- If you have 100 videos getting 1,000 views on average, you have 100,000 views a month

Compare that with your web site! For most people, those numbers are off the charts.

That's why YouTube SEO is critical. Now we're going to show you exactly how to do it.

The Google Bonus

Of course, when most people think of SEO, they think of being found on Google rather than YouTube. The problem is that it's freakishly difficult to actually get Google SEO right. And Google doesn't make it easy, keeping the details of their algorithm confidential as we've mentioned. So Google SEO becomes, at a fundamental level, an ongoing guessing game.

One important parameter for Google SEO is what's called Page Rank. It's a number that Google gives every web site out of 10.

- If your web site has a page rank of 0, it's not good. It's super difficult to get to the top of the results for almost any keyword search term at all.
- If you have a web site with a page rank of 2 or even 4, then you're in better shape but it's still somewhat of a gamble.
- If, however, you're one of the few sites with a page rank of 9, your Google SEO ranking is almost assured.

That means that sites like Wikipedia are always featured in Google searches because they have such a high page rank. Some other high page rank sites include Amazon, LinkedIn and Pinterest.

Of course, Google ranks itself at the very top, then comes Facebook, then comes … drumroll please … YouTube.com.

So what does that mean? It means that it's much easier to rank for a video on YouTube about your special keyword phrase than it is to rank for that same keyword phrase through your own web site. Simply put, YouTube's amazing page rank means it will win *every time*.

Here's what it looks like –

Web   Videos   News   Images   Shopping   More ▾   Search tools

About 186,000 results (0.47 seconds)

Elance Tutorial - A Video Tutorial on How to Use and Hire ...

www.youtube.com/watch?v=FdwXZvaXXeg ▾
Jan 18, 2015 - Uploaded by Tim Levy
This Elance Video Tutorial shows you how to hire people and
about hiring people effectively on Elance.com ...

Elance A to Z or step by step elance | Bangla Tutorial ...

www.youtube.com/watch?v=6bVy4qA2Pdl
May 20, 2015 - Uploaded by Arif Hossin
from this video you will learn how to step by step open elance
account,how to add payment methods,how to ...

How To Use Elance com - YouTube

www.youtube.com/watch?v=Q3VrSTUNAXA ▾
Jun 10, 2009 - Uploaded by Mike Reardon
How To Use Elance.com. ... Elance Full guide ..... Elance
Tutorial - A Video Tutorial on How to Use and Hire ...

Hacking Elance: How To Make $23,700 Freelancing In 4 ...
hackthesystem.com/blog/hacking-**elance**/ ▾
Aug 20, 2014 - So I decided to open up an account on Elance and see if I could start
attracting clients. I knew I could ...... Such a wonderful tutorial. Just when i ...

Elance University | Elance
https://www.**elance** com/q/university ▾ Elance ▾
In this Elance University tutorial, you'll learn how to use Elance's features and tools to
manage your... 0h 04m. Skills: Managing Your Job Level: Watch Now.

[PDF] A Freelancer's Guide to Earning More on Elance.
https://www.**elance**.com/.../**Elance**-Free**lance**r-Guide-March2013.p... ▾ Elance ▾
Whether you're new to Elance or looking to brush-up on your expertise, this ... On
Elance you'll have the opportunity to work with businesses in more than 170

As you can see, we've typed 'Elance tutorial' once again but this time into Google instead of YouTube. Google's search engine algorithm then spits back the following results –

- Firstly, it serves up the paid advertising
- Next, it serves up our YouTube video!
- More videos, then finally, we have Elance.com's own results down the bottom

Do you see the irony, here? Elance's *own results* are ranking behind our YouTube video and its siblings because the page rank of YouTube.com is so high. Elance.com has a page rank of 5 so it's difficult to compete with a page rank 9 site like YouTube.

That's the special bonus of YouTube SEO – it can give you killer Google SEO as a mad bonus! And that drives your traffic up even further.

How does YouTube SEO actually work?

YouTube SEO is an algorithm. So, what does that really mean? It means that there's a computer somewhere that is looking at your YouTube listing, your YouTube video and everything it can see around it to decide where it should rank.

- If you have the best video according to the algorithm, then you rank up the top

- If you have a mediocre video according to the algorithm, then you begin to get lost in the billions of videos that are on YouTube already

- If you have failed to consider YouTube's SEO algorithm at all, then your videos tend to fail to gather search traffic entirely

Our job, then is to understand YouTube SEO well enough to get every video into that first category. In other words, we want our videos to rank! And since *so few people understand that YouTube is an SEO environment at all,* you can do really well.

All SEO works the same way, whether it is Google or YouTube. Let's use an analogy I call the *iron filings* analogy.

The Iron Filings SEO Analogy

Do you remember when you were at school in science class and the teacher pulled out a fistful of iron filings? Each iron filing is a little sliver of iron. Together, it feels like a handful of gritty dust. In our classroom, the teacher would throw these iron filings out onto a white table top and it would go everywhere in a random pattern.

Iron, of course, is a metal. That makes is responsive to a magnetic field.

Next, therefore, the teacher would pull out a magnet and run it past the iron filings (usually underneath the table). Now, something magical would happen. The iron filings would *begin to line up*. They respond to the magnet and each filing magically moves into place. Suddenly, you can see the pattern of the magnetic field and everything makes sense.

So how is SEO like this experiment?

The process of doing YouTube SEO is like running a magnet past those iron filings. When you line up every possible *iron filing* of your video, then suddenly the video's *magnetic field* becomes visible to the YouTube SEO algorithm. If you simply throw your video up on YouTube, then the *iron filings* of your video are totally random and YouTube's SEO algorithm cannot make any sense of it. And that's when your videos fail to attract any traffic at all.

What are the *iron filings* of your YouTube video in this analogy?

The iron filings of your video are the title, the tags, the description and more. We'll get to them in Section Three. For now, I just want you to know that it's our job to line up absolutely everything in the same direction so that the YouTube algorithm knows *exactly* what your video is about and ranks it accordingly.

Does that make sense?! With everything pointed in the same direction, suddenly YouTube can see what your video is all about. YouTube gets on your side and ranks your video higher and higher.

Of course, this isn't unique to YouTube SEO. The same goes for Google and every other search engine. You simply have to line up your iron filings and each algorithm will *get you*. For example, if you get your on-page SEO right for any particular web page, then Google's search algorithm will suddenly understand you and give you a real opportunity to rank. Does that make sense?

Now that we understand what YouTube SEO *is*, we know that all we have to do is line up all those different clues for YouTube in the direction of your video like iron filings in a magnetic field.

- If your video is about blue shoes, every single small aspect of your listing should be about blue shoes.
- If it is about drinking coffee, then everything in your listing should be about drinking coffee.

And when we do this beautifully, YouTube brings the rain to you, your YouTube channel and all your videos.

So, let's stop mucking around and just get into it.

Section Two
Video Tips and Structure

NO MATTER HOW MANY
VIDEOS TOM POSTED,
NO-ONE ANSWERED HIS ADS.

Section Two / Video Tips and Structure

Hopefully by now, you have a good grip on our two key concepts - the importance of traffic and the way good YouTube SEO practices can enhance your traffic.

So, what's next? Why don't we talk about producing your YouTube video? After all, you do have to actually make the video before you can post it, right?

For the most part, I'm going to assume you know the basics of video production. This book is about taking your YouTube mastery skills, and thus your video production, to the next level.

Nevertheless, I'd like to share a few of the shortcuts that have served me well over the years. For my entire adult life, I've been fascinated by video editing. When I was only 17, I created videos for clients like IBM, Dell computers and (the Australian) McDonalds. After a decade of corporate video experience, I went on to produce my own TV show which ran for three seasons on cable and then broadcast TV in several countries. Now we run a digital content agency out of Austin, Texas and what do we love?

Video, my friends, produced as quickly and economically as possible.

Video Production Tips

Tip #1 - The Basics

Video production is quite simple. It boils down to these three key components:

- Shooting your video
- Editing your video
- Making it into a video file that is ready to upload to YouTube

We use the Adobe Creative Suite to edit our videos, which is available for a reasonable monthly subscription. We do everything from editing to sound to motion graphics and effects in the Adobe Creative Suite for around $30 to $50 a month, depending on what options you choose. Students get an even better rate. Given the premium tools the suite provides, this is a tremendously good deal. And if you ever get tripped up, there are a lot of people around (and a ton of great YouTube tutorials) on how to use it.

Having said this, if you'd prefer to produce your videos inexpensively, you can use free solutions like Apple's iMovie or Window's Movie Maker. You can even upload your videos to YouTube and use the editor that's included free in your account!

Tip #2 – Lights, Camera and Sound

Here is a tip you might not expect to hear. YouTube videos do not need to be film or broadcast TV quality. Honestly, when push comes to shove, **you don't need anything more than a cell phone to shoot YouTube videos.** Any of today's smart phones will do! If you can point it and shoot video, you can make YouTube videos. You'll find that iPhones, Android and Windows phones all have incredible cameras.

So how do you make the most of a phone's built in video capability?

1. You should **hold your camera steady**. Moving the camera around makes the video grainy and choppy, making the footage difficult to watch. It also screws up the file compression, which can cause bugs in the process down the line. What's wrong with buying a little tripod? You can

get one for a few dollars on www.amazon.com. Just type in 'phone tripod' and take your pick. Seriously – you can get something delivered to your home (overnight, no less) for less than $20.

2. Make sure you **have lots of light**. Most cameras need lot of light to pick up your picture clearly. Otherwise, in low light situations, the video can get grainy and underexposed. If you're inside, switch on all the lights and when outside, shoot in lovely sunlight. If you need indoor lights, you can find solid LED lighting packages on Amazon for something like $100. Amazing, but true.

3. **Great sound** can separate average from wonderful video. While you can start with the little microphone built into your phone, you may want to invest in something better. You can get one for a few dollars on Amazon. Just type in 'phone microphone' and take your pick. Seriously – you can get something delivered to your home for less than $20. Sound familiar?!

If you're looking to take your gear to the next level and invest in some mid-range video production equipment, I'll get to that next.

Tip #3 – Our Equipment List

So, what might you buy if you have a little more spending cash? People always ask me about the equipment we use, so here's a little list.

- For a camera, we have a few of the Canon Rebel T3i's. It's not the latest model– I think they just released the Rebel T7i. Either way, you can buy one of these for around $500-600 on Amazon.

- Next, I use a little LCD HD 7"to monitor the camera. It helps us frame all our shots and keeps everything in focus. You can grab a Lilliput monitor for less than $200.

- What about sound? Most cameras don't have very good sound. Instead, we record sound independently using Sennheiser wireless microphones (about $600 each) and a Zoom H4N digital recorder (about $200).

- For light, we have a three point LED lighting kit which runs less than $200.

Tip #4 - Location

Location, location, location! Locations are key to a successful video shoot. Here are a few things to keep in mind when choosing locations.

- You need somewhere that is nice and quiet so that you can hear what is being said
- You also need good light, and
- You need a location that is visually rich

If you cruise YouTube, you'll see lots of people don't really take location into account. There are millions of videos shot in people's bedrooms and at dull office desks. We try to pay a little more attention than that.

Our favorite trick is to hire local photography studios and music rehearsal studios. We've found you can get a great studio for something between $20-50 per hour. And sometimes, that price even includes a local crew!

I highly recommend you do a Google search for 'Austin Photography Studio' (substitute your local town or city for the name "Austin"). Austin, Texas is where I happen to be, so that's where I'd search.

Another good trick is to look for band rehearsal space. It's often inexpensive and easily available during the day *when other bands are not playing.* Remember, you need silence to get good quality audio.

It makes a huge difference in the quality of your videos if you're moving into more serious production. Having said that, when you're starting out, your bedroom / kitchen / office will do!

Video Structure

Why Is Structure So Important?

I have to tell you a quick story. It's the story of a huge client with a massive YouTube channel. This particular company had put several hundred videos online and was getting some good traffic.

However, they weren't getting any *conversion.* Do you remember the 3-axis model? When people watch your videos but *don't actually do anything,* you have no conversion. And without conversion, you have loads of potential customers but *no actual clients*. And that, my friends, is a recipe for an unhealthy business.

When we looked into their YouTube channel we found that people weren't doing anything because the video structure didn't allow them to. Simply put, there was nothing to click! How can you expect people to click when your videos don't have any buttons?!

As you can imagine, we then went back to the videos and re-engineered them. So, let's talk about one particular video structure that lends itself to strong conversion results.

When most people post a video to YouTube, they just throw it online. They don't think about it, and they certainly don't think about the structure of the video itself. They pretty much turn on the phone, turn on the camera, take some video and hope for the best.

So, what does good YouTube video structure look like?

The Four Critical Pieces

There are four critical pieces to structuring a YouTube video for optimal conversion.

- First, you need **an introduction that conveys a promise or goal**
- Secondly, it's ideal to have **a lovely motion graphics logo** of some kind (if you can)
- Thirdly, you have the **content** itself, **which will satisfy the goal set in** the introduction. Satisfying the goal generates content that is truly valuable to the viewer.
- Lastly, we have a clear **call-to-action** at the end.

A Quick Example

Before we go into the nitty gritty detail, let's begin with a quick example from my own YouTube channel. We'll use one of my videos on Fiverr which we can all get to online. Let's begin by typing 'Fiverr Tutorial' into YouTube.com. Here's what shows up.

fiverr tutorial   🔍   Upload   Sign in

 Filters ▾   About 86,400 results

Fiverr Tutorial - Video on How to Use Fiverr.com with tips, tricks and secrets in 2014 + 2015
Tim Levy
1 year ago · 49,188 views
In this Fiverr Tutorial, Tim Levy shows you how to use this powerful tool to build your virtual team and make money in your ...
CC

Fiverr Tips and Tricks Video Tutorial - Fiverr.com Secrets for Beginners and How to Use Fiverr
Tim Levy
7 months ago · 3,430 views
Fiverr Tips and Tricks is a video tutorial focusing on the secrets of Fiverr.com. This tutorial gives you fiverr tips and fiverr tricks and ...
CC

How To Use Fiverr Tutorial. Learn How I Make $100 And More A Day On Fiverr
Realtalk101Radio©
2 years ago · 52,450 views
How To Use Fiverr Tutorial. Learn How I Make $100 And More A Day On Fiverr. Fiverr.com for low priced of $5 Learn more about ...

Next, let's click on the second video – Fiverr Tips and Tricks. Immediately, you'll see the introduction which looks like *this*.

The first part of this video is an introduction, lasting about ten seconds. As in this example, your introduction should explain clearly what is to come. Ideally, it should make a promise, and the fulfillment of that promise should be the focus of the content. The promise of *this* video is that you'll learn some special Fiverr Secrets.

Why is this so important? It's important to tell people in the first ten, fifteen seconds or so what they can expect from your video so you can hook their attention. Once you hook your audience, your retention rate will increase. Viewers who are interested in your hook will watch past your intro and are more likely to view the entire video. Remember, retention is important for the YouTube search algorithm. The higher the retention (the more of a video they actively watch) the better it is for the algorithm and your ranking.

Once you've done your intro hook, what's next?

Next comes a motion graphics logo. We'll talk more about *how* to make that happen a little later. You can see it looks a bit fancy. We have taken some time and some effort to create this but I have some short cuts that will allow you to do exactly the same for your own business or product, training or website.

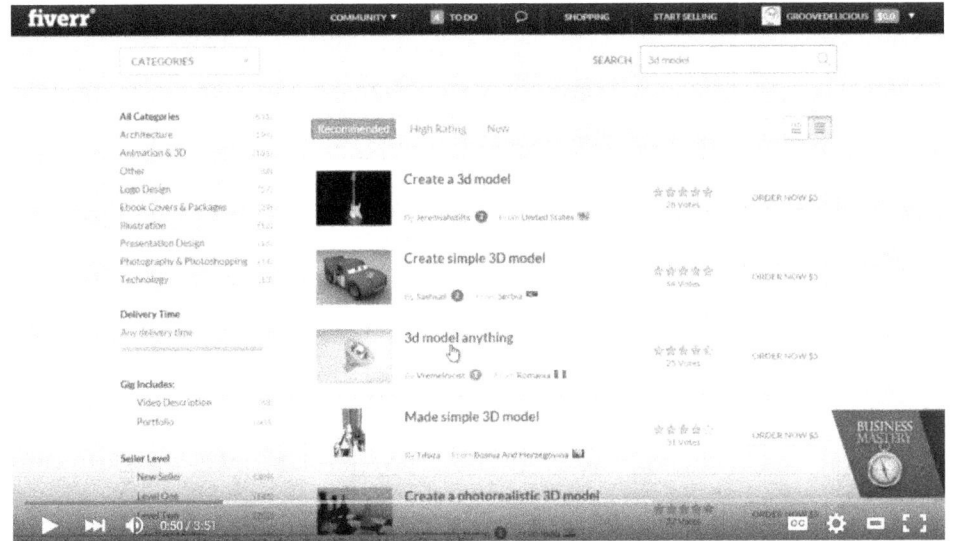

Once the logo is done we have the actual content itself. In this particular video the content goes on for about five minutes.

You can see that in the bottom right hand corner, there's a still logo that sits there the whole time. We call that the *bug* which is similar to the station ID you see in that position on normal broadcast and cable TV. It will turn out to be important later, which is why I'm bringing it to your attention now.

How Long Should the Content Be?

A lot of people tell you there are rules about how long YouTube videos can be. They often tell you that the limit of a video should be 3 or 4 minutes long. I don't agree. We've got videos that are

63

fifteen minutes long and people watch them to the end. **If there is great content, people watch.** That's the real rule!

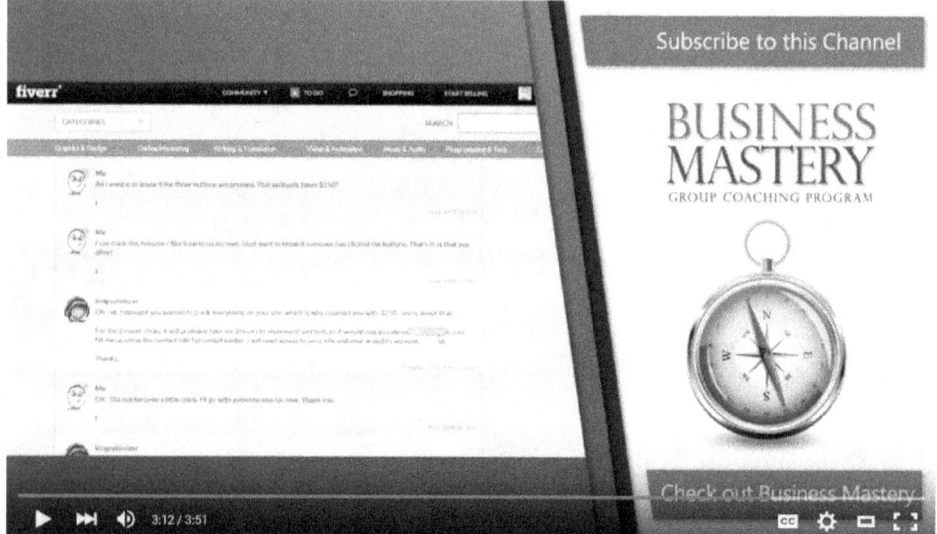

In the last thirty or forty-five seconds of the video we have format changes. The video is shrunk down so you can still see all of it but you have what they call an end-cap, otherwise known as a graphic overlay.

In the overlay itself are some buttons that let you subscribe to our channel. These call-to-action buttons on the right say **Subscribe to this Channel** and **Check out Business Mastery,** the course this video promotes.

A little further down the track the end-cap changes to a full screen overlay. In other words, the main content video has finished and we're now running a graphic for a minute or so at the end. The buttons now say **Subscribe to this channel** and **Visit my site.**

Call-to-action graphics like this are critical to the conversion structure of the video. Without them, there's nowhere to put a button unless you use YouTube's ugly overlays (which we like to avoid).

Then we fade to black.

That's the overall structure.

1. Start with an intro

2. Cut to a motion graphics logo

3. Move into your valuable content

4. Follow with your call-to-action end-caps

Let's consider these four structural areas in detail.

Section One – The Introduction

The first piece should be your **introduction,** also known as your **hook.**

The hook should ideally be ten to fifteen seconds long and explain to your audience in a concise manner what's to come. When you *don't* begin with a quick, clear summary of the content, viewers tend to go somewhere else for the answers they're looking for.

It's easy to notice this behavior by looking at your YouTube analytics and checking your retention curve. If the curve slashes downwards in the first 10-30 seconds, then you haven't hooked the viewer in. If this happens, you may want to redesign your introduction! If your retention curve simply moves gently into the content, then you're in good shape.

Here's what a good curve looks like –

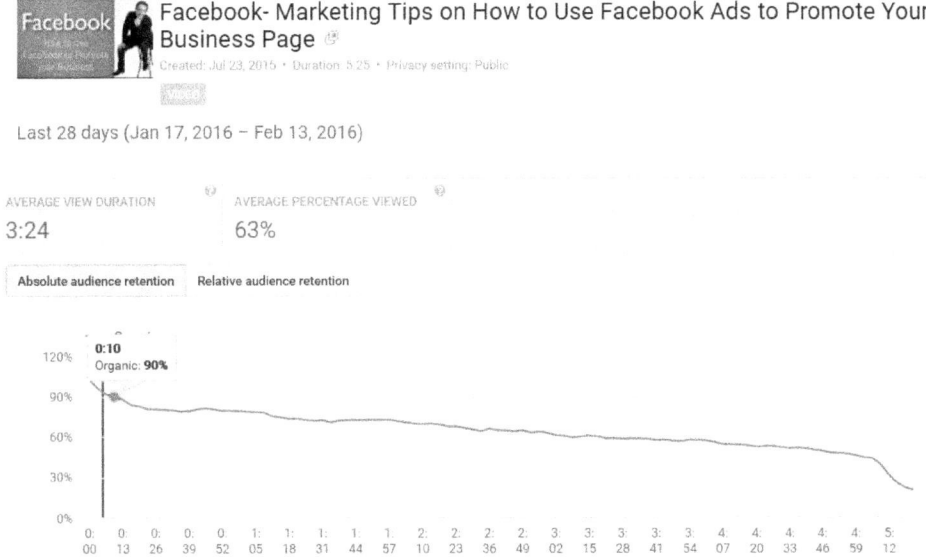

This is the retention curve for a video with a strong hook, indicating the video has a high retention rate, and is thus valuable content on Facebook marketing. You can see that after 10 seconds, we still have 90% of our audience. The curve slopes down gently which means that most people are watching this video almost completely through until the end. The video dips at the end when we introduce our call-to-action end caps – which is fine.

Here's a bad curve –

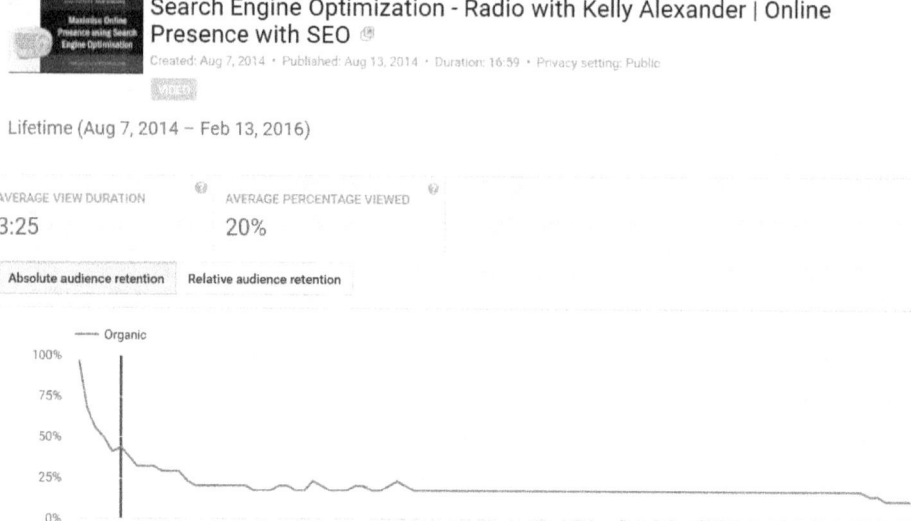

Search Engine Optimization - Radio with Kelly Alexander | Online Presence with SEO

Created: Aug 7, 2014 • Published: Aug 13, 2014 • Duration: 16:59 • Privacy setting: Public

Lifetime (Aug 7, 2014 – Feb 13, 2016)

This video has no hook whatsoever. It was a video experiment that did not work. We simply took a radio interview and cut it into a video with a single image holding for 16 minutes. It turns out people don't like that kind of thing and the video has clearly flat-lined. Who knew?!

So, make sure you do a quick introduction with a compelling hook which explains to viewers what's to come in an energetic and fun way.

Section Two – The Logo

The second section of your video should be a **logo** of some kind. In an ideal world, you would have some lovely motion graphics with your gorgeous logo incorporated within.

Why is this so important? It's important to use high quality motion graphics where you can because it screams *quality*.

What I mean is that people are used to seeing motion graphics on television every day. Therefore, if you create lovely motion graphics that look like television, your video will be perceived as a high-quality production, *whether it is or it isn't!* It's amazing how good even terrible footage can look when you put lovely motion graphics at the beginning and end of it.

The great news is that while we used to have a huge motion graphics teams create a simple asset, we can now actually create beautiful motion graphics for as little as $5. I'll explain exactly how in the section just around the bend called **Doing the Magic**.

For now, let's look at what comes after the opening logo.

Section Three – Content with Bug

The bulk of any video should be the actual **content**. Whether the video is two or five or fifteen minutes long, it doesn't seem to make any difference **as long as the content delivers real value**. Many people will tell you emphatically that your videos should have a certain length; our experience leads us to another conclusion.

The success or failure of a video does not rely on the length at all. Instead, it's about the genuine value of the video. In other words, the video must make a beneficial contribution to the viewer's life.

- Does your video give valuable information?
- Does it make the viewer laugh?
- Is the video entertaining?
- Does your viewer get something out of it?

Once you've found a way of communicating genuine value, you won't have to worry about the length of the video.

Having said that, once you have an established audience, you must again consider _conversion._ How can you structure your content for conversion?

The answer lies in what is called the *station bug or sometimes station ID* when you're talking about television.

So, what is a station bug? Well, have you ever noticed that whenever you're watching TV there is always a little station logo in the lower right hand corner of the screen? They put it there so that you always know what channel you're watching. You'll see it on CBS and NBC and ESPN. Now you know what to look for, you'll see it everywhere!

Sometimes it's the full logo. Sometimes it's a little transparent so it doesn't interrupt the show you're watching, *but it's always there.*

So, let's make sure to create our own station ID or, as they call it in the industry, station bug. It's part of the video structure we'll need once we've posted on YouTube.

So how do you do it? You simply create your own station bug image in a graphic program like Photoshop. Then you composite the graphic over your content section when you're editing. It's simple for any editor to do. Again, we're assuming you have strong knowledge of the editing process or that you're working with an editor who does.

Then, once you're in YouTube, you can create a spotlight end screen to make it an active, clickable button. More on that process, later. For now, just remember to put in a bug!

Section Four - Call-to-action

The **call-to-action** comes at the end of the video. After all, once your viewer has watched the video, you want them to actually *do* something, right? That's what the process of conversion is all about.

This call-to-action is also sometimes referred to as the **end cap** or **end graphic.**

So, what are some of the conversion actions we might ask our viewers to do? It could be:

- Subscribe to my YouTube channel
- Visit my website
- Buy my book
- Make a phone call
- Engage in my business or my project

So how do you manage this? Well, it's the same idea as the bug. You simply create a graphic using a program like Photoshop, then overlay that graphic at the end of the video.

Here are two interesting options we often use: full screen and video overlay.

- The full screen is simply a full screen graphic that you edit on to the end of your video. The graphic should incorporate button graphics with clear calls to action so that the viewer knows they're being asked to click directly onto the video. Here's another example of how this might look.

The video overlay leaves a section of the screen available so that the video can actually continue, just at a smaller size. You simply limit your call-to-action graphic buttons to the other areas of the screen. Here's an example how that might look.

Whatever it's going to be it should look like a graphic that is on screen so that later we can overlay it with a button using YouTube's annotation technology. More on that, later.

Note – YouTube is changing its annotation technology. You'll need to check on their site for the latest updates.

That's how you convert the video from something people just watch to something where they take real action and engage with you or your product or your business.

Recap

That's everything you need in your video structure. Let's look at it one more time:

- An **introduction or a hook** that promises something interesting, engaging and of genuine contribution to keep the viewer watching
- An opening motion graphic **logo** to make everything look professional and high quality
- A wealth of **valuable content** with a bug over the top
- A **call-to-action** converting the viewer from passive observer to actively engaged with you, your project or business

Of course, there are a variety of ways to alter this structure but I suggest you make sure you incorporate these sections as a bare minimum. From there, be creative!

Doing the Magic

Of course, some of the things we've spoken about seem difficult or even impossible. After all, not everyone is a professional graphic designer, video editor, motion graphics designer or YouTube programmer. So how do you accomplish all of this?

Let's talk about how you can do all this magic and here's the big secret. You don't! You can easily and cheaply outsource a lot of these tricky tasks through a web site called www.fiverr.com.

> You can see a quick video tutorial online at http://www.timlevy.net/fiverr.

And just to make life even easier, I'll share another little piece of magic we use all the time, a web site called VideoHive.com.

> You can see a quick video tutorial online at http://www.timlevy.net/videohive.

Fiverr.com

Back in my TV days it used to be insanely expensive to design graphics, produce motion graphics and edit. It cost tens of thousands of dollars per episode and we produced dozens of episodes each year!

These days you can utilize a website called www.Fiverr.com where these tasks can be outsourced at the base cost of five dollars. Here's what that web site looks like at the time of publishing this book.

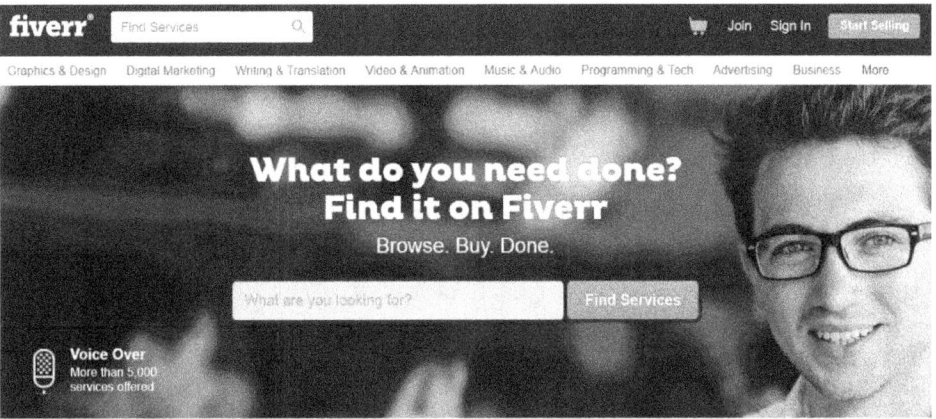

Of course, it'll be a little different when you read this book, since it changes every day.

What is important here is that you can get an insane variety of tasks outsourced here for as little as five dollars at a time. OK – I must correct myself here – they recently started charging sales tax. So technically, I think a gig costs $5.50 but you get the idea.

Thank you, my beta-testing people for pointing that out! When you're doing hundreds of gigs each year as we are, that 50 cents can add up!

There are some options for upsells as well, so you can extend the basic job (or gig as they are called on Fiverr).

For example, if you want a sketch done of a dog, a simple line drawing might cost you five dollars. For ten dollars, you might get the shading done. For twenty, you might get full color with a background. If you want to use the sketch for commercial purposes, you might pay ten or twenty dollars for the commercial rights. And so on. The point is, it is always clear how much you will pay for each step, and you *can* get that simple unshaded sketch for five dollars.

So how do we get those amazing motion graphics, bug design or even video editing done? You can simply search the web site for appropriate gigs.

I just typed in **video logo** to find motion graphics experts. Fiverr tells us that there are over one thousand gigs available. Here's the beginning of the list –

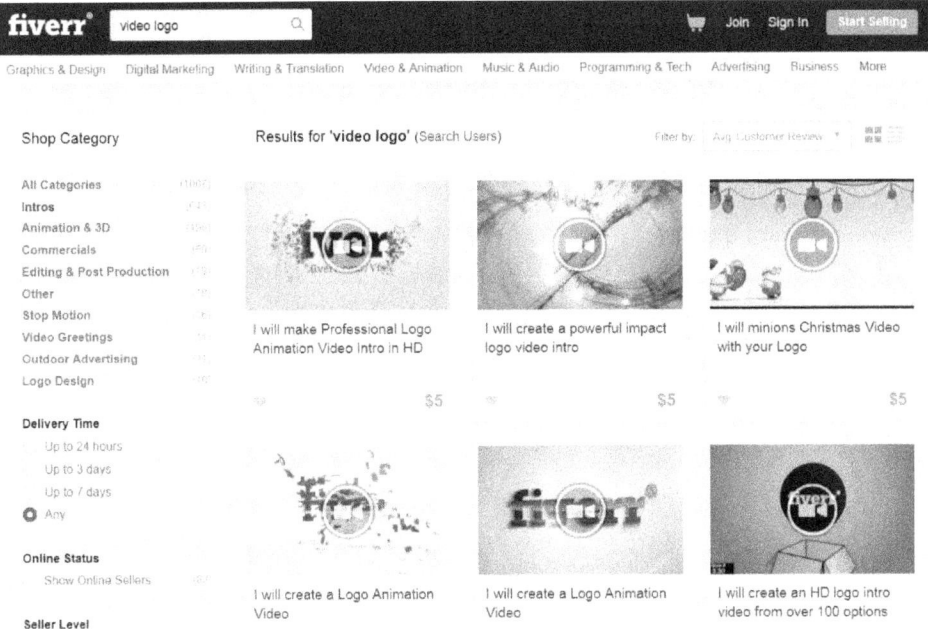

If you give someone five dollars, they will go away and put your logo and your words into these 3D animations and send it back to you generally as HD video, ready to use. Amazing, right?!

Let's see what happens when you click on one of these – in this case, the first one in the list.

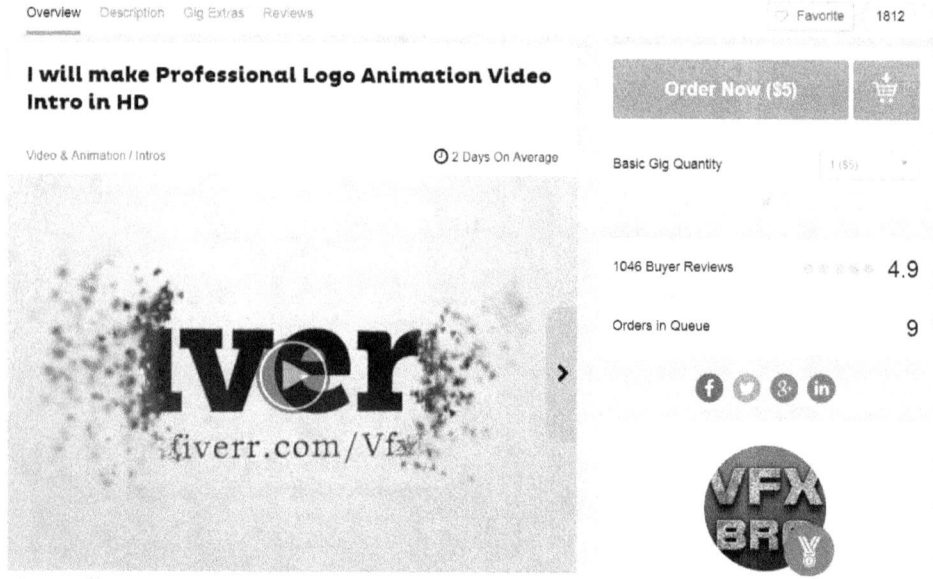

As you can see, this person will make you a motion graphics logo
for $5. Seriously.

Also, you can see that this person has 1046 reviews! That means
this gig has been done over 1000 times already and retained a 4.9-
star rating! That's a good sign that this animator does great work.

This kind person would insert your logo and web site URL into
the motion graphic and send it back to you, done. The animator
will configure everything for you, your business, and your videos.
For five dollars a pop you can have terrific graphics.

It's magic, right?!

Of course, you don't have to type in 'video logo'. What if we type in Photoshop designer? Here's what pops up.

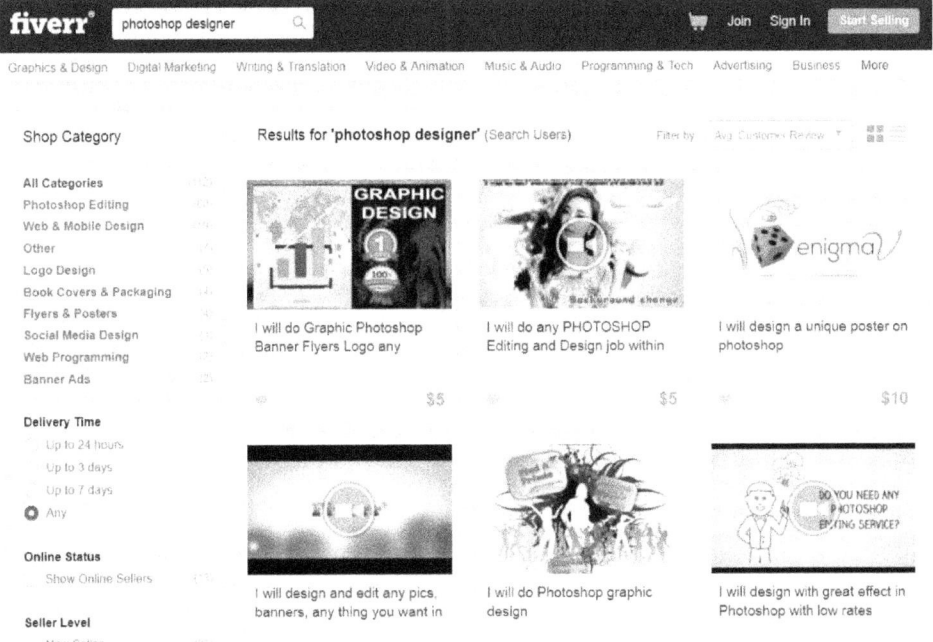

There are more than 100 Photoshop designers here to help, starting at $5! Or what if we type in video editor? Here are the results Fiverr generated today.

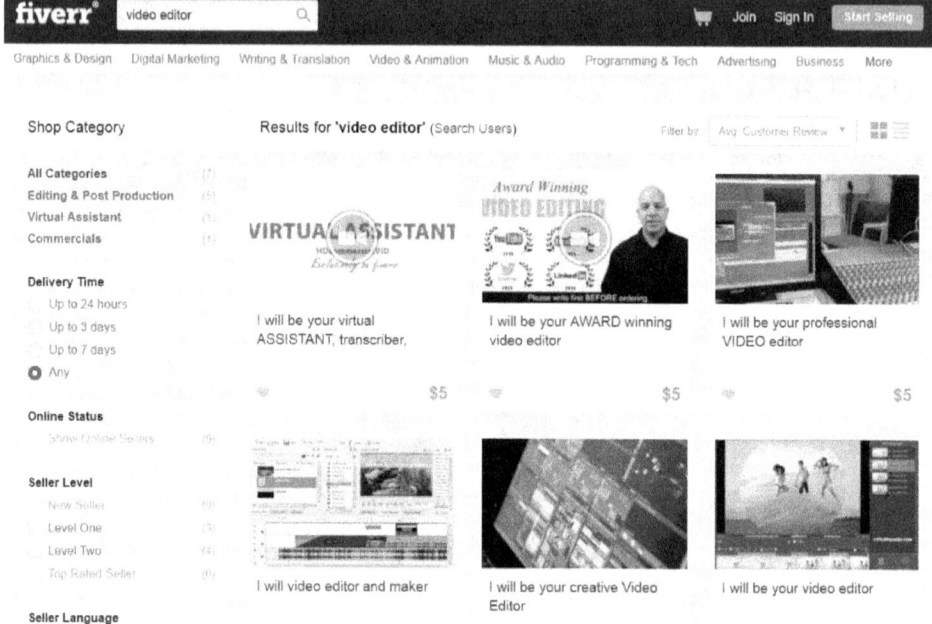

There are your video editors, starting at $5. It's an amazing site.

If you'd like more detailed information on how to build amazing online teams using platforms like Fiverr.com, I have another resource for you.

You can grab a copy of my book *The Entrepreneurial Handbook* with this link – www.timlevy.net/handbook.

Videohive.Com

There's one more magic tool I'd like to introduce before we leave our conversation about video structure. This is a web site that is an amazing resource for video motion graphics, video stock footage and more. It's called **www.videohive.net** and I highly recommend it.

Here's how it works. Let's start with how it looks:

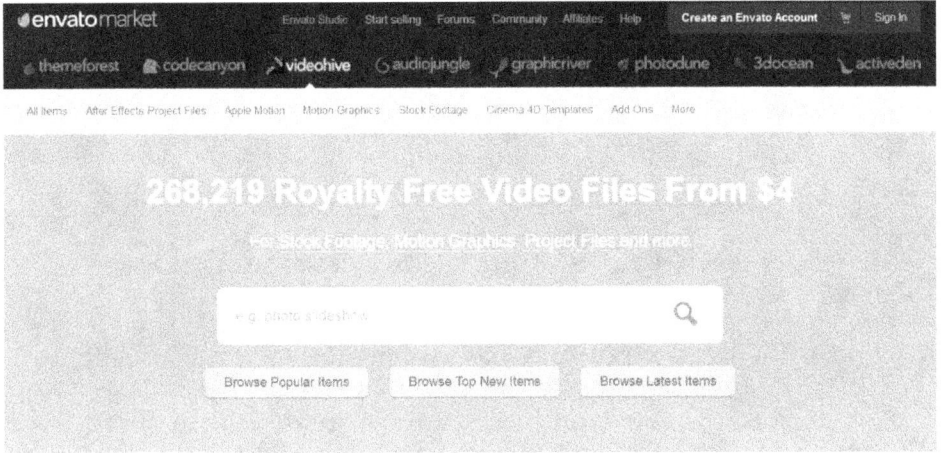

OK – so what do you do from here? If you'd like to buy an amazing motion graphics package, I'd suggest you type **broadcast package** into the search box. Here's what comes up:

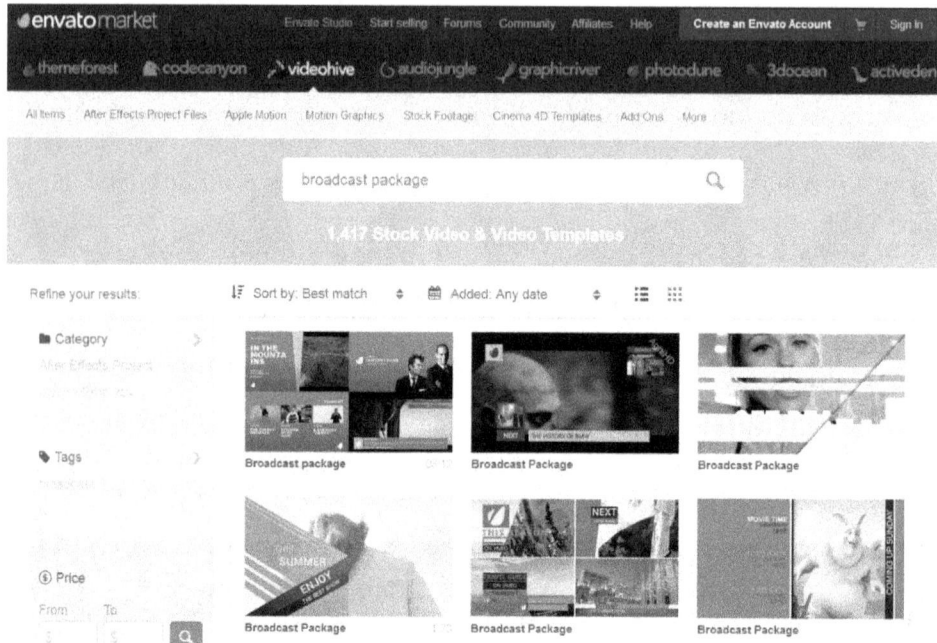

As you can see, there are over 1400 search results. So, you'll need to narrow it down! Before we do, what *is* a broadcast package?

A broadcast package not only has an opening logo but usually a whole lot of other bits and pieces thrown in as well. In short, it gives you everything you need to generate the motion graphics for a broadcast channel. In our case, however, we're going to use these assets for YouTube videos.

Just click on any of the packages to see a short video trailer of what you're going to get. You can narrow the results down by specifying price or category or other tags. In other words, you could try 'broadcast package news' for pieces that look like the motion graphics from the evening news. You could try 'broadcast graphics cooking' if you're producing videos about cooking.

We buy a different motion graphics package for each YouTube channel we have. They're usually about $30 to $60, which feels like a super bargain price, right? Especially when you remember we had to spend tens of thousands of dollars to do the exact same thing back in my television days.

Each package generally comes as an **After Effects** project so you can edit it yourself. That means you can change the graphics, tweak the colors and put your own logo into the render. If you don't know how to use the Adobe After Effects program, it's not a problem, because you can go back to Fiverr.com and find someone who knows how to use After Effects! I still find the whole process magical. It's so easy and so inexpensive! And you get amazing, professional results.

Those professional designs, motion graphics and edits make your videos even better. And we've found that high quality videos tend to be viewed more often (traffic) and clicked on more often (conversion). It makes sense, right?

Now that you understand our key concepts, along with video structure and how to produce your content with beautiful graphics, it's time to *get all your material ready to post.*

Section Three

Getting Ready to Post

I DON'T CARE HOW MANY HITS IT'S GOING TO GET, WE'RE NOT CALLING OUR DAUGHTER "HOT CHICK 2016"

Section Three / Getting Ready to Post

Now everything is getting ready to come together. By the time you've reached this point, I'm assuming you've got a clear understanding of traffic, conversion and the 3-Axis model. I'm assuming you've read all of Section One and that you understand what YouTube SEO *actually is*.

I'm also assuming you've read Section Two on video tips and structure. That means you should have at least one well-structured video standing by, ready to post on YouTube.

Here, in Section Three, we'll get everything ready for your first YouTube SEO friendly post. There are five steps we'll explore with this in mind –

1. Hunting for Keywords
2. Transcribing the video
3. Designing a thumbnail
4. Optimizing the filenames

Here's a screenshot of my preparation folder for a video about 123RF – which is our example video for this process. It's a video about a website I mentioned earlier caked 123rf.com, the one where you can get low-cost high-quality graphics.

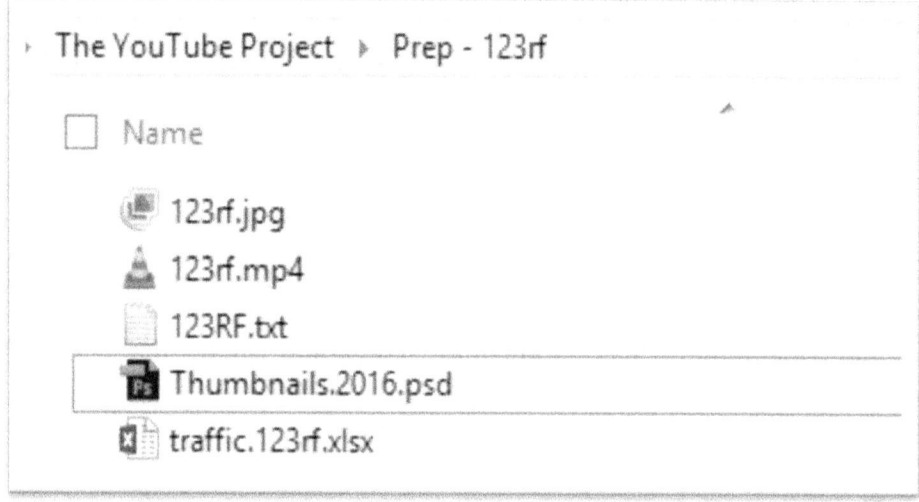

This folder already has everything ready to post. It has the following files –

- 123rf.jpg – the thumbnail
- 123rf.mp4 – the video we're going to post
- Thumbnails.2016.psd – my thumbnail template in Photoshop
- Traffic.123rf.xlsx – my Excel file to track search results

So let's go back to the beginning. How do we build all of these things?

Step 1 – Hunting for Keywords

When our video is ready, we need to search for keywords. To do this, please open an empty spreadsheet in Microsoft Excel. Type at the top 123RF keywords (only of course you'll use the title of the video you're putting up).

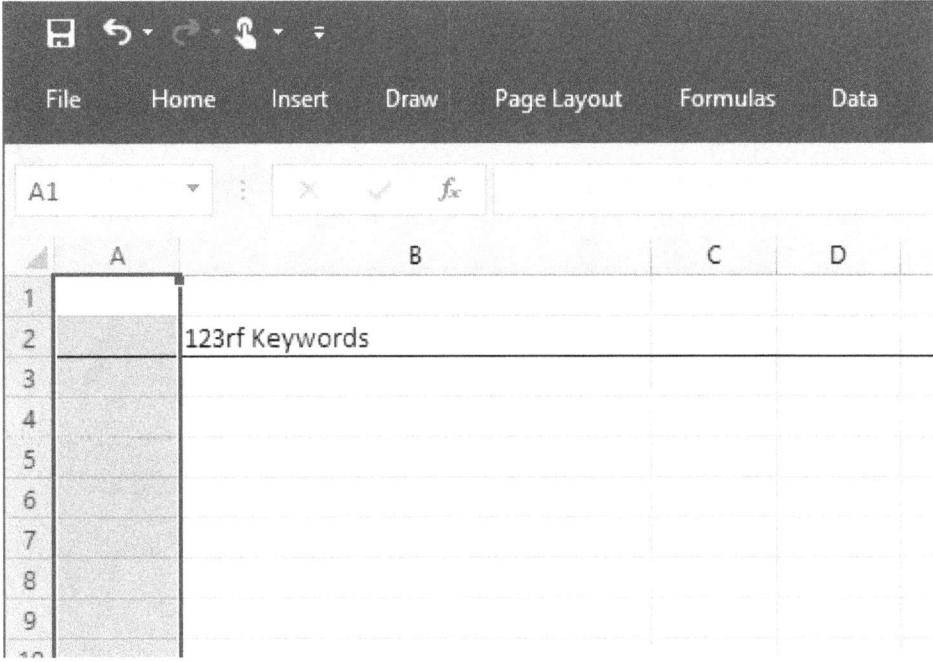

Next, let's jump in and look for keywords using YouTube.

Using my example, which is about the website 123RF.com, where we buy royalty free graphics, I type keywords into the spreadsheet through guesswork. So, **royalty free graphics** is obviously one of those keywords (a keyword can be a phrase). **Free graphics** is probably helpful, and so is **low cost graphics**. I know 123RF creates photos, so **low cost photos**, is one, as is **photos**.

123rf Keywords

royalty free graphics
free graphics
low cost graphics
low cost photos
photos you can use

That's just a bit of groundwork before we flip over to where we really find the best keywords. To narrow down our keywords, we open YouTube.

Go to YouTube and do not log in. Either log out, or open a browser you don't normally use for YouTube. Type keywords into the search box and take advantage of **YouTube's autocomplete function**.

In other words, as you start to type words into the search box, YouTube auto-completes the term, which indicates where the most traffic is going. For example, to find out if there's traffic around 123RF, I go back to YouTube and I type '1', which is the first character in '123RF'.

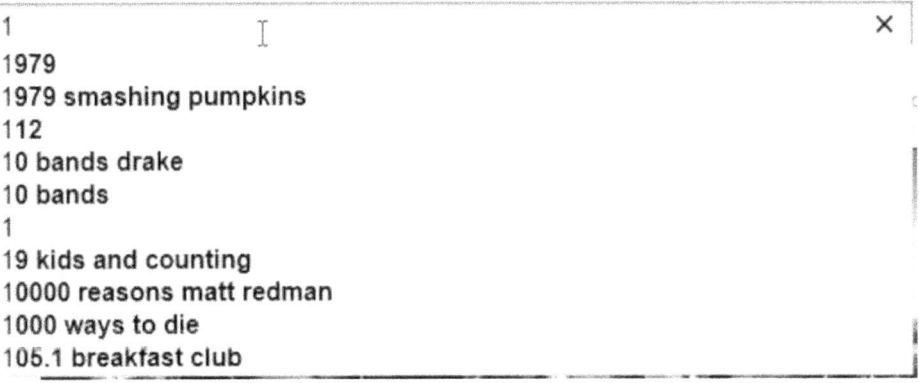

As soon as I begin, you can see the search dropdown begins to populate with what YouTube considers to be popular. So, we see there's traffic around 1979, Smashing Pumpkins, 10 bands Drake, 1000 ways to die and 105.1 Breakfast Club among others.

None of those is relevant to me, so I ignore them all and keep typing. When I have '123' things start getting interesting but none of the options look like my website.

```
123
123 song
123
1234
123 victory
1234 wallpaper
123 victory kirk franklin lyrics
1234 plain white t's
1234 feist
1234 get on the dance floor
```

So, on to **123r**. There is a little bit of traffic for the keyword **123RF**. This is what I want.

```
123rf                    I                              ×
123rf
123rf free
123rf tutorial
123rf upload
123rf gratis
```

So, I now know that there's 123RF traffic, there's 123RF free, 123RF tutorial and 123RF upload. I'm not covering 123RF upload, as it's irrelevant, so I'll ignore that. I'll take 123RF free and I'll take 123RF tutorial. Now I'm beginning my list here of keywords in Excel.

123rf Keywords

royalty free graphics

free graphics

low cost graphics

low cost photos

photos you can use

123rf

123rf.com

Just by using this, we can start again now on **royalty free graphics**.

So, let's start typing in our key words, and take note of the auto-complete search results. It looks like there's some traffic for royalty free graphics.

Filters ▼ ⠀⠀⠀⠀⠀⠀⠀⠀⠀⠀⠀⠀⠀⠀⠀⠀⠀⠀⠀⠀ About 74,400 results

Get Royalty Free Images With Google Images
by Ming Jong Tey
2 years ago • 212 views
Download proven BKH Blueprint for Free http://www.mingjongtey.com/go/yt5-bkh.html
◄◄◄ to kick start your online business
CC

How to legally get 10 million royalty free images
by Lindsay Heuton
2 years ago • 3,537 views
Get Free Stock Photos here http://bit.ly/getfreestockphotos Take a look at my videos
and go to my site to help you with free stock

Get royalty free images. I wouldn't have thought of that. **How to get royalty free images**. That's nice, too.

123rf Keywords
free graphics
low cost graphics
low cost photos
photos you can use
123rf
123rf.com
123rf free
123rf tutorial
royalty free graphics
royalty free images

How about **low cost graphics** or even **cheap graphics**? Let's look at this. **Cheap graphics, cheap photos, Photoshop, cheap images**. I'm trying to find where there would be good traffic for this.

Now, since I'm a little stuck, I'll look up 123RF.com in YouTube and look around.

123rf.com

by 123RF.com
1 month ago • 18,084 views
Your creativity is calling. Your need to express a feeling, capture a moment, or convey an idea. So you work tirelessly to realize

HD   CC

Como Descargar Imagenes Gratis de Internet, Google y 123RF.COM
by Leonardo Vera S
8 months ago • 4,480 views
Skype adsensechile / Facebook http://facebook.com/leoveranet Twitter http://twitter.com/leoveranet / Web

123RF.com Quickies - Introduction to the world of Stock Photos
by 123RF.com
3 years ago • 2,931 views
This 123RF.com Quickie introduces one to the concept of stock photos, broad licenses for stock photos (Royalty Free and Rights

HD   CC

They've got their own channel, which is helpful. I'll look there for some ideas from some of their own videos. **Stock photos**. That's probably what I'm looking for. **Stock** – and there it is, the mother-load. All those are fantastic for me. I can grab a screenshot of that.

97

| stock ph| | ✕ |
| stock photography |
| stock photography tips and tricks |
| stock photos |
| stock photography tutorial |
| stock photography business |
| stock photo video |
| stock photo license commercial use |
| stock photography sites |
| stock photo music video |
| stock photography ideas |

Stock photography, stock photos, stock photography tips and tricks. What else have I got? Stock portfolio is no use. Stock photography tutorial – that's good. Photography tutorial. You can see what's happening here; we're building up a list of keywords about stock photography sites. These keywords are relevant to that one video.

I tried other keywords, such as **photos you can use**, but they weren't good. As soon as the autocomplete doesn't complete, we know there's no traffic there. There was nothing for **low-cost photos**, or **low-cost images**. Trying these isn't a waste of time; it helps rule out the words that are a waste of time.

And here's where we wind up –

123rf Keywords
123rf
123rf.com
123rf free
123rf tutorial
royalty free graphics
royalty free images
stock photography
stock photos
stock photography tips and tricks
stock photography tutorial
stock photography sites

YouTube is kind enough through its autocomplete system to show you what people search for. Once I have a selection of high-traffic keywords, I save them in an Excel spreadsheet, ready to use for the upload. This is everything I need to do to prepare the keywords to upload to YouTube.

Step 2 - Transcript of the Video

Now we have our video in the correct format, and we have our keyword research. We secured keywords based on using YouTube's autocomplete function to find where there's existing traffic, and what people are already searching for. If we can rank for those keywords then we get beautiful organic SEO traffic from YouTube free of charge, which is lovely.

It turns out that YouTube is unable to watch our video to see what it's about – since it's just an algorithm, right? So, it looks for clues in places like the titles, the description and tags.

Where else does the algorithm look? The algorithm looks at your transcript or closed caption. Many people tend to overlook this last bit, but we are going to dive into it here. A closed caption is simply the transcript of all the words in your video. It's the only way YouTube has of truly knowing what you're talking about in the video!

If you do not create a closed caption, then YouTube takes a guess, sometimes to highly comic effect. In other words, YouTube doesn't always get it right but *it believes that it does*. So, without a closed caption, you're leaving YouTube to rank you on that guess. Instead, let's do the work!

Firstly, we need to prepare a transcript of our video. While you can of course transcribe your video yourself (simply watch the video and type the words using Microsoft Word or Notepad), it's a lot easier to outsource this task.

I prefer to use a shortcut and that involves employing someone from fiverr.com. (Remember Fiverr? That's where you can purchase animated logos.) Fiverr is one of my absolute all-time favorite amazing tools on the Internet.

In this case, the keywords we type into the search box at Fiverr.com are **video transcription**. Let's see what pops up!

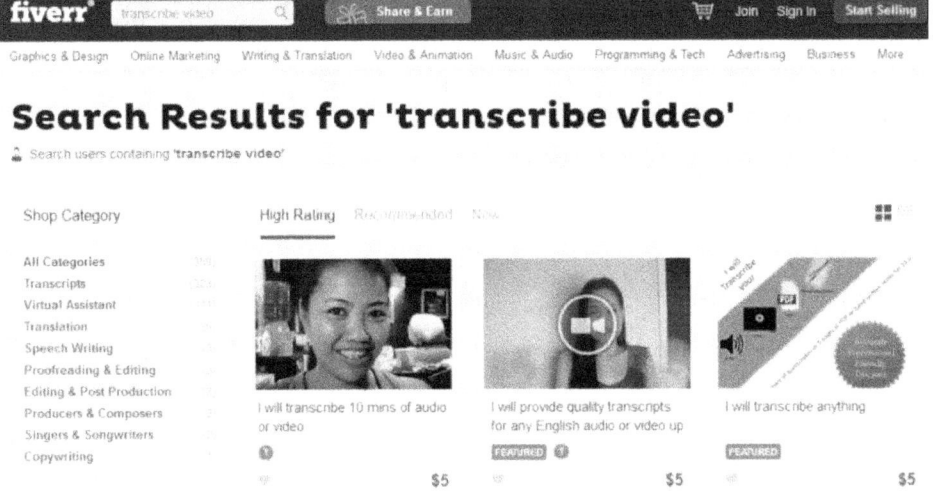

I found more than three-hundred people offering to transcribe video. One person I've used before is called Debbie. If you look at her statistics, you see she has five circles in her score, which means excellent ratings. Secondly, she's completed more than 1K jobs, so more than 1000 times she's done this gig. She'll transcribe 10 minutes of audio or video for $5, which is fantastic.

Now, I wouldn't necessarily hire Debbie to do a job today, because, if I look at her statistics I see she has forty-seven orders in the queue. I wouldn't want to wait for her to get through forty-seven other orders, so I'd find someone else who has a good rating, a good track record, but a shorter queue. I might find someone who will do fifteen minutes for a fiver, or eighteen minutes. I'd also look at the time-frame. One person has sixteen orders in queue, and twelve days' return. That's a bit slow. Another one has a five-day turnaround. That's better. Someone else has a three-day turnaround, and this person offers eighteen minutes of translation, and offers additional options, such as extra fast delivery.

If I'm in a hurry, that's terrific. I also look at reviews from the past, and they're good. When I've chosen someone, all I have to do is click "order now" and send the person a link to my video or if the video hasn't been uploaded, which it hasn't, I send them the video directly. I like to use Dropbox, a web site used for transferring large files.

You send your Fiverr worker the video and it comes back with a transcription. What does that look like? Here's one. It's the transcript for 123RF, prepared as a text file. That's important. You don't want it as a MS Word file; you want it as a text file.

Where do you go to get to great images for incredibly good deals? 123RF, it's our secret go to place for images costing as little as a dollar. Check it out in this video. Alright, I want to talk to you today about a neat little tool that we use when it comes to graphics. When it comes to photos and images in particular. Now we use this all over the place in business, from presentation materials to blog posts. It's a website called 123rf. Now, it used to be back in the day that we used other websites for this. Websites like the getting images sites, iStock, but they because stupendously expensive. So, we started using 123rf instead. I'll just log in here so I can show you what this is about. It's very easy. All you need to do is if you need an image on any particular topic, you type it into the search bar here and the images show up which you can then buy. That's easy. So what would you use the images for? Well, let me give you an example here. One of them is in our blog. When we have a blog post we like to add an image to it. Let's have a little look here, for example, at something recent. And you can see here, for example, here's an image about 15 minute break-through. It's a clock with a 15-minute timer on it. So, let's see. Here's one about fear. Here's one about a solution. You can see all these different ones here. Here's one about snoring. So let's see if we wanted to have a blog post on that. That one's actually an image that's a thumbnail of a YouTube video, so it's a little different. But let's have a little look at an image here if we wanted a 15-minute breakthrough. How would we find that image? Well, if I type in 15-minute breakthrough, it's not going to automatically pull up a clock. Although, it did pull up some interesting things. Look there. There's a clock idea. There's another clock idea. Oh look, it actually probably did. So that's probably working. I don't why I found that one pretty quickly. If I type in just 'breakthrough' it's going to come up with a bunch of breakthrough ideas. Fantastic. And if I type in 15 minutes, it's going to come up with other ideas. OK, good. So, let's say we like this one here as a timer and I click on that. What it's then going to tell me is how I can buy it. And as long as I'm not planning to sell it again, which I'd need a different kind of license for, I can use this standard license. And the way this thing works is with credits. So, how do you buy credits? Well, at the moment you can see I've got 13 credits just sitting there in the system. And a credit is around about a dollar-a-go. But lets just go and see if we can grab some credits on 123rf. I always find it confusing when I went to find this but otherwise it's down at the bottom here and hit this one where it says "buy credits". And you can see here you can either get a daily subscription or you can download a pack. Well I don't use either of those. I use this one here where it says "On Demand". So I'll download 20 or maybe 40 dollars at a time. What you can see is the more you spend, the cheaper the credits are. But in general I consider them to be worth around about 1 dollar each. So if I come back to here and I've got that image we were looking at, all I need to do is select the level that I need, the resolution that I need, and you can see here these top 2 resolutions are for web use. So that's perfect for a blog post. I click on "download" and it'll show up saving it onto my computer, ready to use for the blog post. One little tip, you might want to rename the actual file for your blog post to give you a little boost when it comes to SEO. So when you for example, upload this image here or that one there, instead of leaving the name to whatever the file is when it comes from 123rf, you might change it to 15minutebreakthrough.jpeg to have a little bit of SEO relevance to your blog post. Neat little tip there. Either way, I highly recommend 123rf. One other feature which I really like is their "like" boxes. This allows you to collect groups of things together. So for example over here you can see a collection I made when I was trying to figure out the title page for one of my presentations which was about ideas and I wound up using, I think, this one here. Other "like" boxes that I have, one of them I know has a whole lot of Prezi backgrounds that I use for creating Prezi presentations. And you can choose to make those ones shareable, which means they're public, or you can choose to make them private. I usually keep them private. Occasionally I share them with one of my clients. So, that's another helpful feature in 123rf. But either way, a great place to buy images inexpensively for your business.

As you can see, it has no formatting. I like to open it up very quickly, just to make sure there are no glaring errors: for example, 123RF is spelled correctly. That's good because it's a keyword.

OK, so now I have my transcript.

Step 3 – Designing a Thumbnail

The next thing I need to get ready is the thumbnail. If you don't get a thumbnail ready, then YouTube just makes a guess and picks a random frame in your video. That frame generally not optimized for conversion, which is to say it's just a random picture and it doesn't draw people to the video.

Instead, it's best to build my own thumbnail that's going to look fantastic and draw people to click the button. An attention-grabbing thumbnail is critical in getting people to watch your video.

I have a thumbnail template that I've built in Photoshop. Here it is.

Elance

How to build a cheap, effective virtual team.

If you put together a thumbnail template like this – and you can use any graphics program, I just happened to use Photoshop— then it's easy to make quick changes. For example, in this template I've used a photo of me. I used it for a video for a site called Elance. If I want to change that, all I have to do is change the word Elance. So, how do I do that?

I click on the word *Elance*, and change it to 123RF, which is the website we're talking about in this sample video. I'll also change the tag language to "how to get cheap royalty free images." Now the image is prepared, I'll save it as **123RF.jpeg.** Here's the result.

Thumbnails from Fiverr

If you're new to Photoshop, there are other ways to create images. The first thing I'd recommend is to go to our favorite website for things like this, which is Fiverr.

Fiverr is good for many things, including design. If we type in **thumbnail design** or maybe **YouTube thumbnail**, several options come up.

There are many sellers who say they create YouTube thumbnails, and plenty of others who do general design, including logos. They could probably create thumbnails too. You could search for example, just general design. So, I've taken it back to general design and you can see these people will create logo designs, so chances are they'll do thumbnail design for you as well.

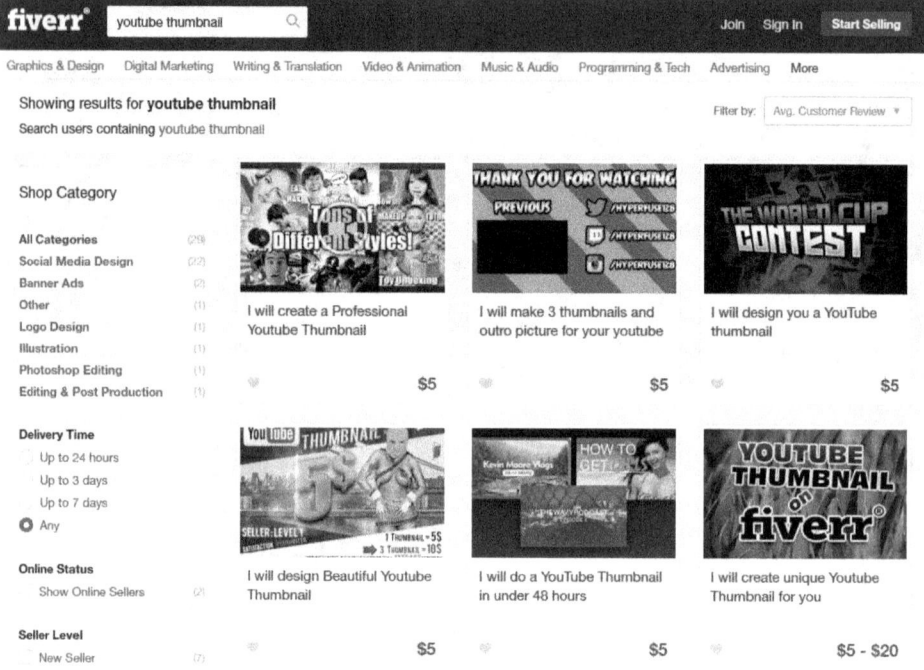

If I look at one of the two thumbnail designers and the examples look good, you should look at the designer's turnaround time. Some designers have an incredibly quick turnaround time – some will produce your logo for you for five bucks and you'll have it back, ready to use, in three days' time.

Thumbnails from Graphic River

The second thing I suggest is another website called Graphic River. GraphicRiver.net has templates for thumbnails. These are previously established graphics you can easily edit. If you look on this website for thumbnails you can see that people have already made some.

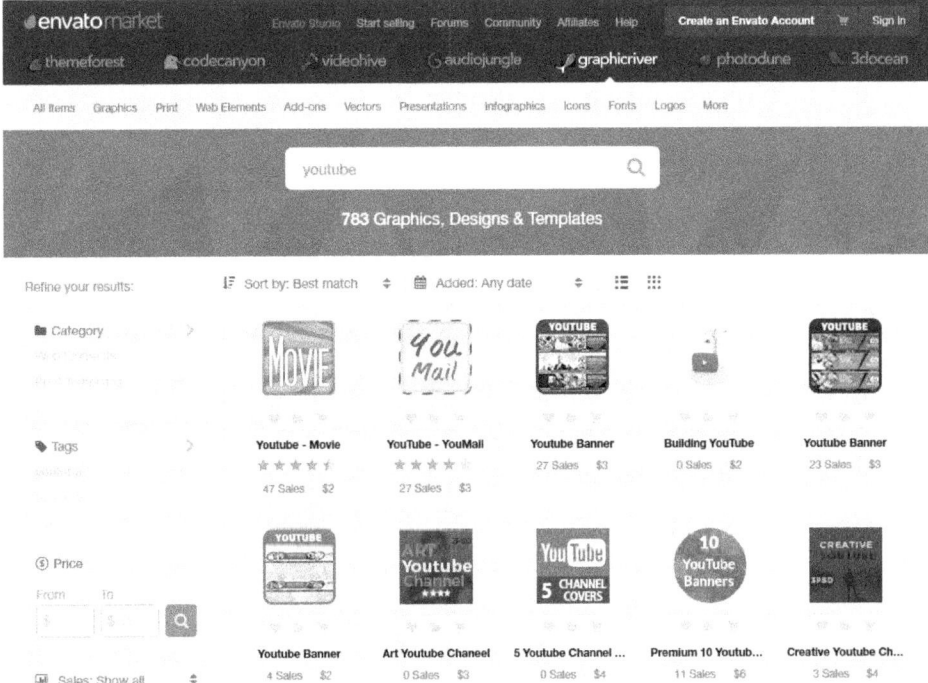

You can buy templates for YouTube banners, thumbnails and other artwork for just a few dollars.

Step 4 – Optimizing Filenames

Now we are nearly ready to post to YouTube. We've got almost everything we need.

- We've got our video with the appropriate structure
- We've got our keywords sitting over here in Excel
- We've got a closed caption text file with all the words, ready to upload
- We've got ourselves a thumbnail

Now, remember, YouTube is looking everywhere for clues as to what this video is about. So, what we do now is load the file names of the closed caption, the video itself and the thumbnail with the keywords we're interested in. How do you do that?

123rf Keywords
123rf
123rf.com
123rf free
123rf tutorial
royalty free graphics
royalty free images
stock photography
stock photos
stock photography tips and tricks
stock photography tutorial
stock photography sites

Let's look at that video I've been using as an example. The spreadsheet is full of keywords I found by hunting for keywords that were (a) relevant and (b) already driving traffic. Now I will combine the most popular terms to create our title.

Firstly, my title must have the word **123RF**, because that's what the video is about and adding 123rf**.com** makes sense here, too. If I just use 123RF it's not clear to everyone so I'll add in **royalty free graphics**. The word **images** is important. So is **stock photography**. Then there is **video tutorial**. It's a little bit long but it includes most of the keywords we're looking for; **123RF**, the word **free**, the words **tutorial, graphics, images, stock photography**.

So why not smoosh them all together and you have '123rf.com royalty free graphics and images and stock photography video tutorial'. That's our title!

Now we have our title ready to use as a file name jam-packed with all our keywords. All I need to do is copy that and rename the thumbnail with that keyword rich title I just came up with. Then I can do the same for the MP4 and the same for the text.

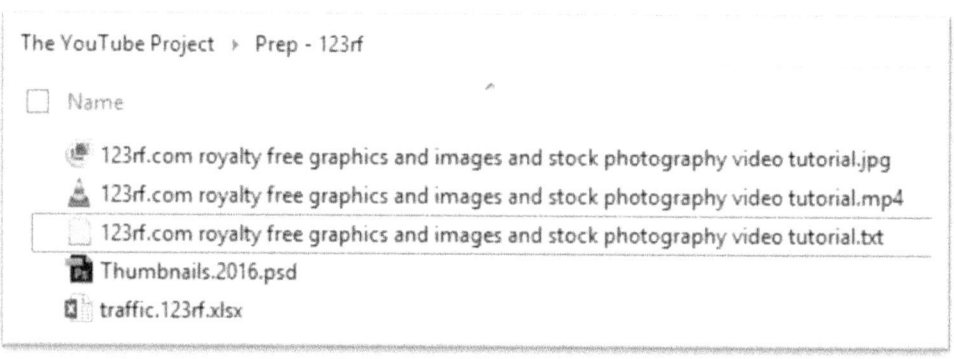

The result is three files to upload to YouTube, to tell it exactly what I'm going for; all those keywords, and that particular .com. I'm telling it that in three different ways.

Now I'm finally ready to upload to YouTube.

Recap with another Example

Before we go further, let's look at what's been done so far.

Before posting video, we need:

- A video
- A closed caption
- The keywords we're going to need
- The thumbnails
- And they all need to be titled correctly

Just to make sure this is all clear, I want to go through it again, using another example.

Let's say I have a second video to post, based on a website called VideoHive. Videohive.net is a great website where you can go to get stock video footage as well as templates for motion graphics. It's very handy!

Here's what we're aiming to build – the thumbnail, the video, the transcript and the Excel file to track our results. Oh – and you'll see I have the Thumbnail template there again, which is in Photoshop.

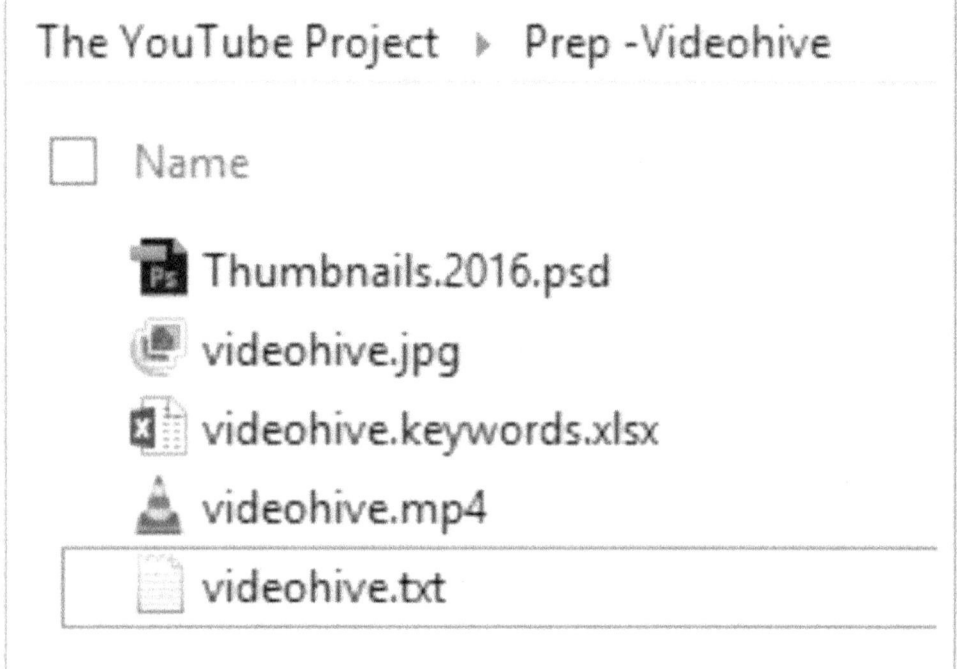

Firstly – we must Hunt for Keywords.

How did we hunt down the keywords? First, we thought of some keywords that _might_ be useful.

So, this website is called **VideoHive**, so I'm hoping I'll get that web name as a keyword. Maybe I could use **VideoHive tutorial**. Now, I can tell you what VideoHive is about. It's about buying templates that are pre-populated in software like After Effects. I might write **After Effects templates** and hope for some traffic there. I think you can get **Photoshop templates** there, and maybe **Motion Graphics templates** and **Broadcast graphics**.

VideoHive Keywords

videohive
videohive tutorial
after effects template
photoshop templates
motion graphic templates
broadcast graphics

The next step is to go into YouTube (making sure we are signed out) and start autocompleting keywords, using the autocomplete technology in YouTube to find out what some of the already-busy keywords are.

If I type in Video H for hive, straightaway we've got a hit. VideoHive After Effects template is the one I want. What comes up? VideoHive tutorial, video-holic, VideoHive After Effects project files, VideoHive templates and VideoHive flat design.

```
videoh|
videohive
videohive after effects template
videohive tutorial
videoholic
videohive - after effects project files - flat design
videohive templates
videohive flat design
videoholic 90sb
videohahahas
videoholicultimate
```

I'm going to use VideoHive templates and VideoHive flat design. Next, I find VideoHive presentation, and VideoHive After Effects, which is the one I was looking for. So I put all of them in my list in Excel. Here's what it looks like now – all ready to go!

VideoHive Keywords

videohive

videohive.net

videohive tutorial

videohive.net tutorial

after effects template

motion graphic templates

broadcast graphic templates

videohive after effects template

videhive templates

videhive.net templates

videhive flat design

videohive after effects

videohive movie reveals

videohive movie trailer

videohive openers

after effects template tutorial

Secondly – Get a transcript

The next thing you might recall is to get a transcript of the video. Remember what we did? I went to the website fiverr.com and typed in **audio transcribe**, and sent off the video to a transcriber to have it transcribed for five dollars. When the file came back I made sure to check the main keywords for correct spelling.

Thirdly – Get a Thumbnail

Next, I need a thumbnail. As before, I'll use my existing template and edit it a bit. **VideoHive, Motion Graphics** and **After Effects templates**. I save the file as a JPEG once again, renaming it as VideoHive.jpeg.

Finally, Optimize Filenames

Now that I've got my thumbnail, my keywords, my closed caption and my video, now all I need is a title that encapsulates all of that, utilizing the major keywords. I'm certainly going to use the word **VideoHive**.

How about '**VideoHive.net tutorial Motion Graphics and After Effects Motion Graphics templates**, **movie trailers, plus broadcast graphics'**

This is a long name, but it gives those keywords. **VideoHive, tutorial, Motion Graphics**, **Broadcast, templates** and **After Effects** are all there.

The YouTube Project ▸ Prep -Videohive

☐ Name ⌃

Thumbnails.2016.psd

videohive.keywords.xlsx

Videohive.net Tutorial - After Effects Motion Graphics Templates + Movie Trailers + Broadcast Graphics.jpg

Videohive.net Tutorial - After Effects Motion Graphics Templates + Movie Trailers + Broadcast Graphics.mp4

Videohive.net Tutorial - After Effects Motion Graphics Templates + Movie Trailers + Broadcast Graphics.txt

And we're ready to post!

Section Four

Posting the Video

"YOU ARE FILMING THIS RIGHT?
THIS SHOULD GET US EPIC HITS"

Section Four / Posting the Video

There are four parts to posting the prepared video to YouTube.

1. Upload your **video**. This is simple after all that preparation.
2. Fill out all the boxes, in particular the ones marked **title, description** and **tags**. Again, you've already prepared all this, so it's easy to do.
3. Upload your **thumbnail**.
4. Then hit the **publish** button.
5. A couple of seconds later, add the **closed captions** (using our transcript file).

When you follow all those steps correctly, you have your best possible chance of ranking your YouTube video.

Step 1 - Uploading

Now we come to the interesting part where we actually put everything together and upload to YouTube.

The first thing we need to do is to go to YouTube.com and sign in.

Click on the blue button on the top right of the page to sign in. If you're not already a member, you can create your own free account. Remember, YouTube is owned by Google, so you must login using a Google account – or create a new one.

Google

One account. All of Google.

Sign in to continue to YouTube

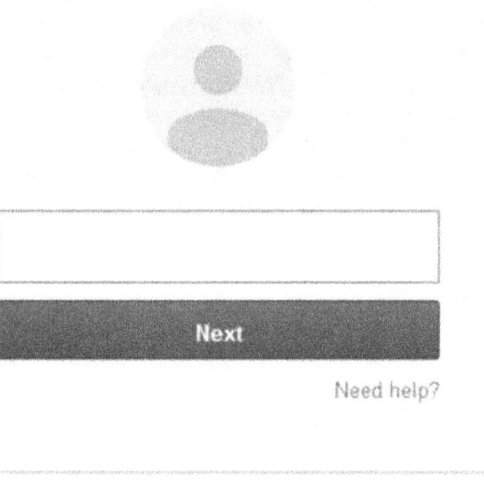

Next

Need help?

Create account

One Google Account for everything Google

I use an automatic sign in password system for all my websites called LastPass, which you can look up. You can go to LastPass.com or go to YouTube and actually type in **LastPass tutorial**, and you'll see a tutorial about how to use it.

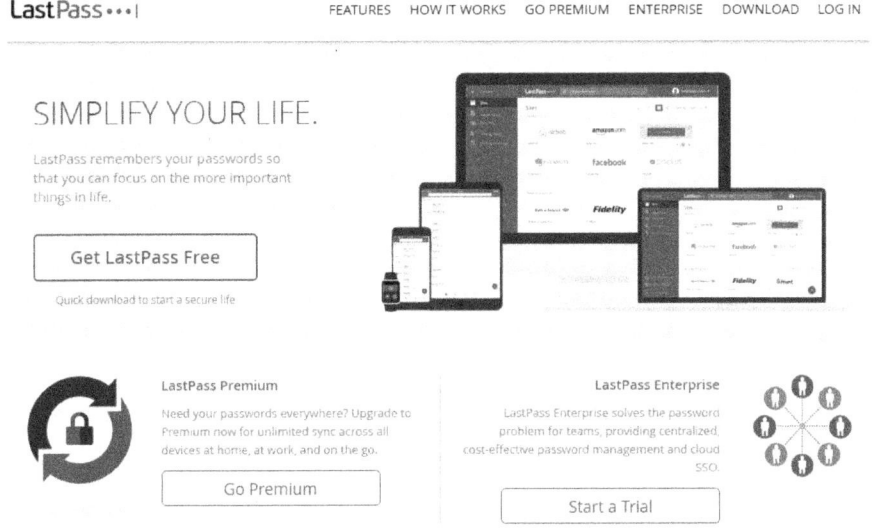

All we need to do now is click on the upload button.

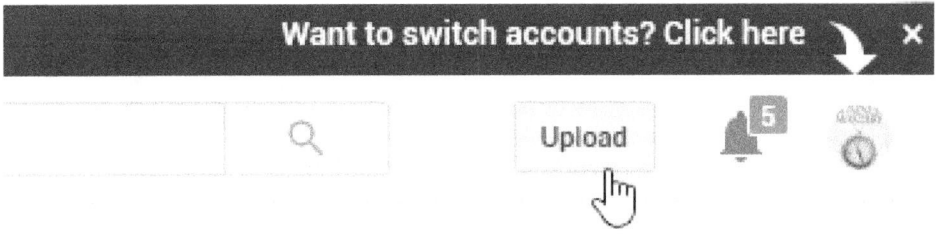

YouTube is now ready for you to upload your video, which we have ready. You can drag your video into the window or select the file by click on the arrow.

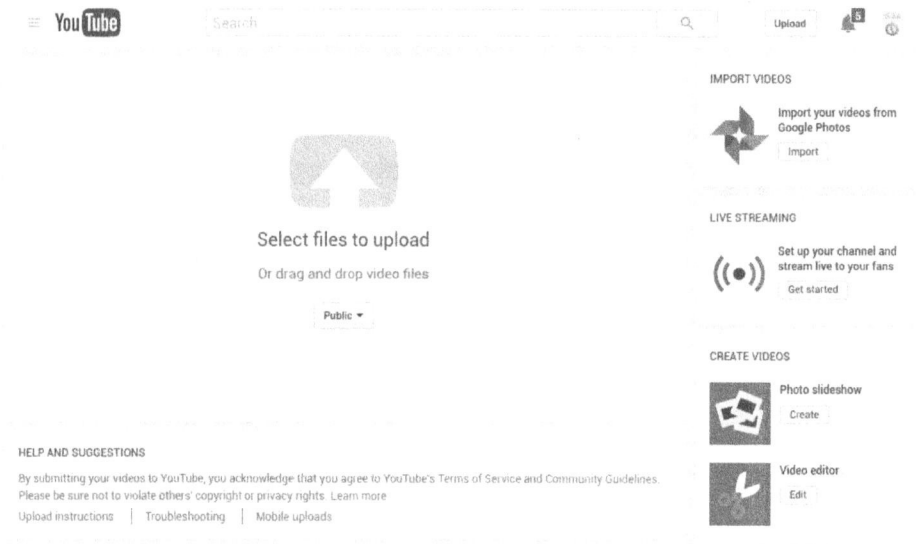

Uploading is easy. YouTube tells you how much time is remaining. It also tells you up on the left what the URL's going to be. **Don't** hit **publish** right away. There's more to fill in first.

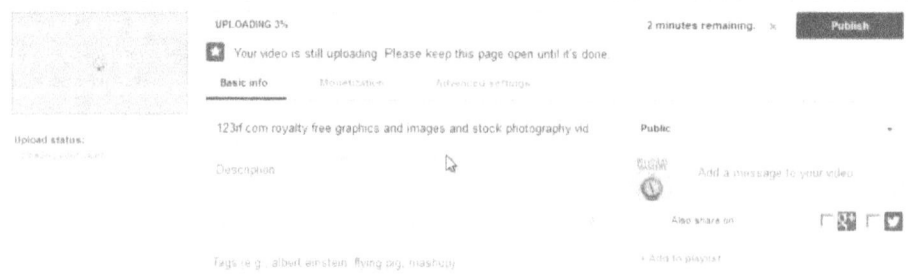

Step 2 - Filling in the Fields

Now we need to fill in three fields.

- The **title** field
- The **description** field
- The **tags** field.

Title Field

You may find the title field has already pre-populated from the file name. In the example you can see it already says **123RF royalty free graphics**. I just had to capitalize some of these keywords and add the words **video tutorial**. Our title is already inputted, because we prepared the file name.

Tags

Next come the tags. Tags come straight out of our keywords, which we already prepared.

They just need to be pasted in one at a time.

I use control-C to copy each one and control-V to paste it. There is a limit to how many tags YouTube will register, so input them in order of importance. As you go, YouTube will suggest some keywords. In the case of the 123RF video, YouTube suggested **Royalty free, tutorial, graphics, free** and **photography**.

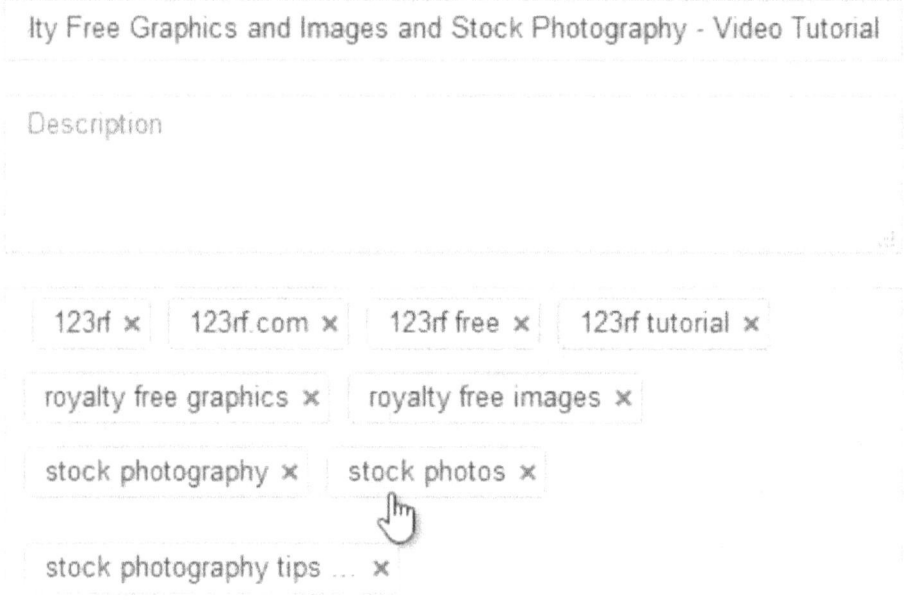

Description

The next thing we have to input is the description – this is where it gets interesting. This is really the only challenging part of this operation. **We need to write two or three sentences, incorporating all my keywords.** I have to use all of these keywords in those first two or three sentences. This is mission critical. For the 123RF video, I might start with this:

This video about 123RF is for people who need royalty free graphics and royalty free images.

Now I want to use the '.com' so I continue like this:

123RF.com is a website offering super cheap graphics, photos and photography.

Now I flip back to my keywords and continue:

This stock photography tutorial shows you a fantastic stock photography site.

I've just used these key words and sentences, **royalty free graphics, royalty free images**, then **123RF tutorial.** I've got three sentences incorporating all the keywords.

lty Free Graphics and Images and Stock Photography - Video Tutorial

This video about 123rf is for people who need royalty free graphics and royalty free images. 123rf.com is a web site that offers super cheap graphics and photos and stock photography. This stock photography tutorial shows you a fantastic stock photography site

Adding a Bio

The next thing I might do is include a short bio about myself. I can include something about myself or about our website.

The bio gives you a sense of who I am and what I'm about. Note there is hardly a limit to the length of this description, but best to keep it concise and to the point.

I'm also adding a light call-to-action – asking people to **visit us at our web site.** You can see the end result here -

This video about 123rf is for people who need royalty free graphics and royalty free images. 123rf.com is a web site that offers super cheap graphics and photos and stock photography. This stock photography tutorial shows you a fantastic stock photography site.

VISIT US ONLINE
Please visit our web site - www.timlevy.net - for more books, videos and information.

ABOUT TIM
Tim Levy is an author, speaker, consultant and coach working with CEOs and entrepreneurs on clarity, strategy and mindset. He routinely speaks for leading organizations like Vistage International, CEOSpace International and Secret Knock. His clients consistently report transformational shifts and rapid growth in their business and personal lives.

There are two last things I want you to do.

1. The first thing is to write **Keywords** and then go over the Excel spreadsheet and cut-and-paste all your keywords here as a list.

2. And the second thing to do is grab the URL of the YouTube video we're going to post and put it down at the very bottom. You can get that from the YouTube screen you're posting to – it's on the left hand side. You can simply cut and paste it in.

Your eventual result looks like this -

VISIT US ONLINE
Please visit our web site - www.timlevy.net - for more books,
videos and information.|

ABOUT TIM
Tim Levy is an author, speaker, consultant and coach working with
CEOs and entrepreneurs on clarity, strategy and mindset. He
routinely speaks for leading organizations like Vistage
International, CEOSpace International and Secret Knock. His
clients consistently report transformational shifts and rapid growth
in their business and personal lives.

KEYWORDS
123rf
123rf.com
123rf free
123rf tutorial
royalty free graphics
royalty free images
stock photography
stock photos
stock photography tips and tricks
stock photography tutorial
stock photography sites

http://youtu.be/gyysu0Y6CTI

Now we have a complete description. We're still not ready to
actually hit that publish button though!

Steps 3 - Publishing the Video

We're now nearly ready to publish this video. You've noticed that uploading and publishing are two different things.

1. **Uploading** means just dragging and dropping the video
2. **Publishing** means hitting the blue button on the top right.

What we have accomplished up to this point is uploading the video with our selected keywords in the name. We've got that keyword rich title in our title; we've got our description where we've loaded those first couple of sentences with keywords; and we have our call-to-action, the keywords themselves and a link back to the video.

Don't forget, down at the bottom of the screen, there's a section addressing **custom thumbnail**. We want to make sure we input our custom thumbnail, remember?

VIDEO THUMBNAILS

Thumbnail selections will appear when the video has finished processing

Custom thumbnail

Maximum file size is 2MB

It's there waiting in the folder, already named. It's very easy to see that our custom thumbnail (along with our keyword heavy title) is ready to go. We click open, and it uploads.

There is one caveat here – what if the thumbnail button doesn't appear for you? It means you haven't verified your email with YouTube. So go and check your email inbox to see if YouTube has sent you an email – it comes when you open an account. The email will have a *verify* link inside – click it and your thumbnail button will appear.

Now we can hit that publish button. The Video is already in YouTube's database. Hurray! Your video is now online and YouTube can begin sending your traffic.

There is, however, one last magic step we'll take to optimize your listing. We're going to use your transcript to add closed captions to your video.

Step 4 - Closed Captions

Once you've published your video, you can add closed captions. The option is not available until you've published the video. So how do you do that?

Now, I hit my top right channel icon and go to the Creator Studio.

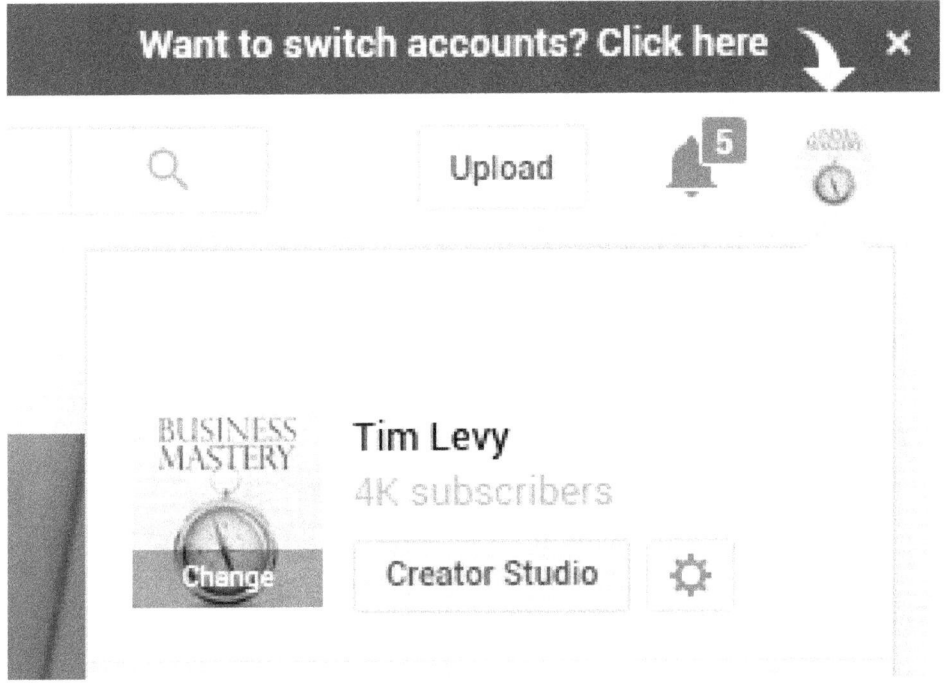

I wind up in my dashboard. Now the video I just uploaded is listed as the latest video. If I click on the little drop-down button now, the possibility of going to subtitles and closed caption has suddenly emerged.

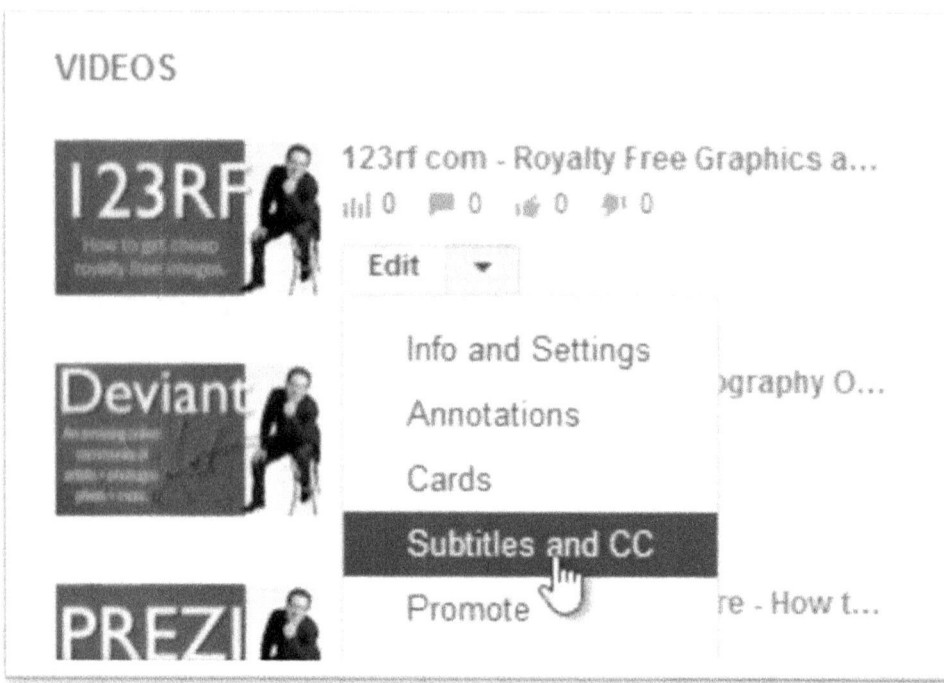

YouTube will now try to do an automatic English transcription. The YouTube version can be spotty and unreliable. Luckily, we've got ourselves ready. I already have the transcription I had done on fiverr.com.

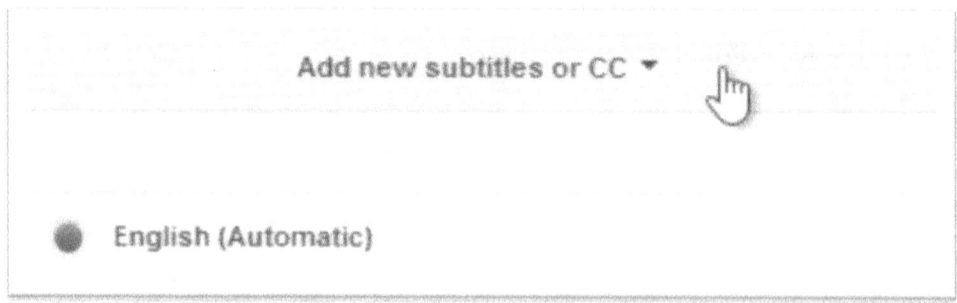

I click on **add new subtitles**, and I want to add one in English. The option comes up to **upload a file**. Well, as you know, we are more than ready here. I click on **browse** and there is our text ready to go, so I hit **upload** and up it comes.

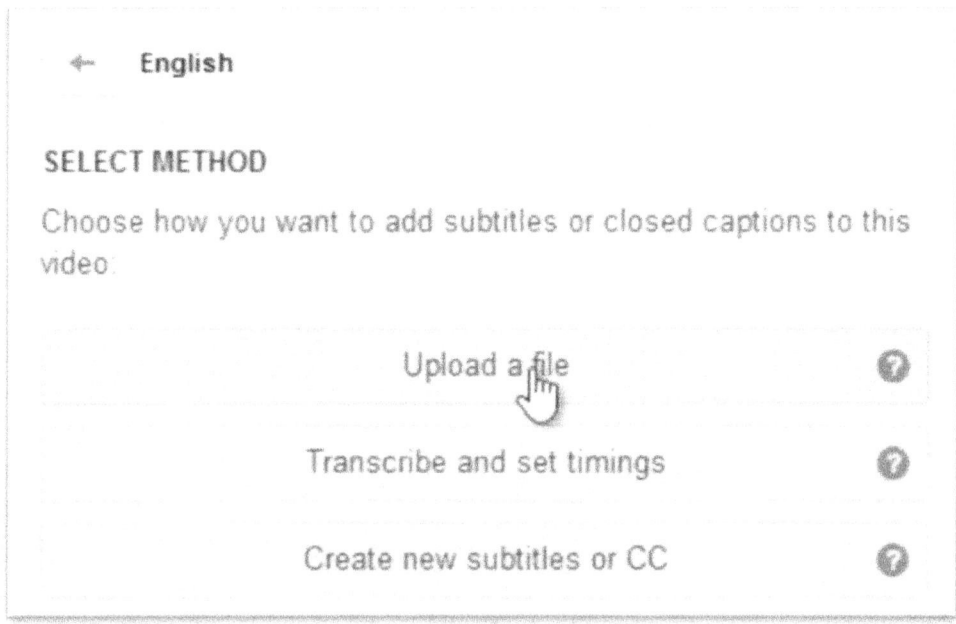

Setting the Timings

Next I have to ask YouTube to set the timings.

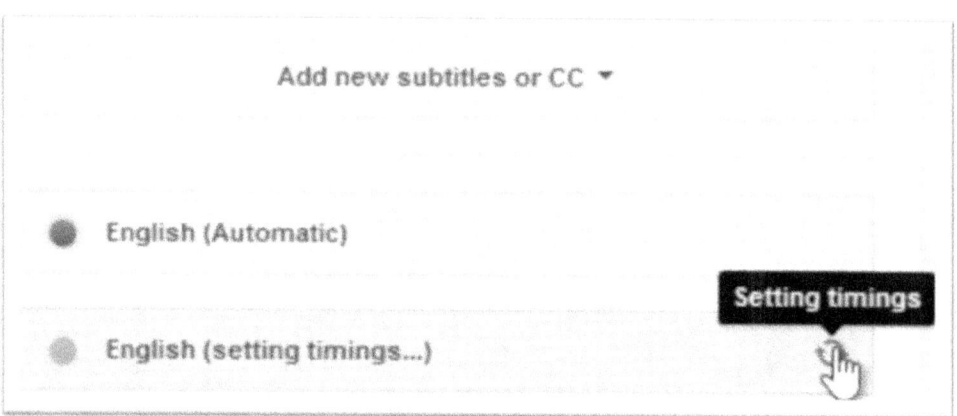

That means, YouTube is now going to go through the video and match the text that we gave it to the actual words. If I hit the button where it says **set times** at this point, it's going to say to us, **Listen, I'm still doing this, just give me a moment**. So, you have to give it a minute or so to get that right and then you'll be able to publish. So, let's wait a second and give it that opportunity.

What you'll see is that the little round button is no longer there. That means it has figured out where the timing is. Down in the very bottom corner now is an option to publish that. Hit that immediately.

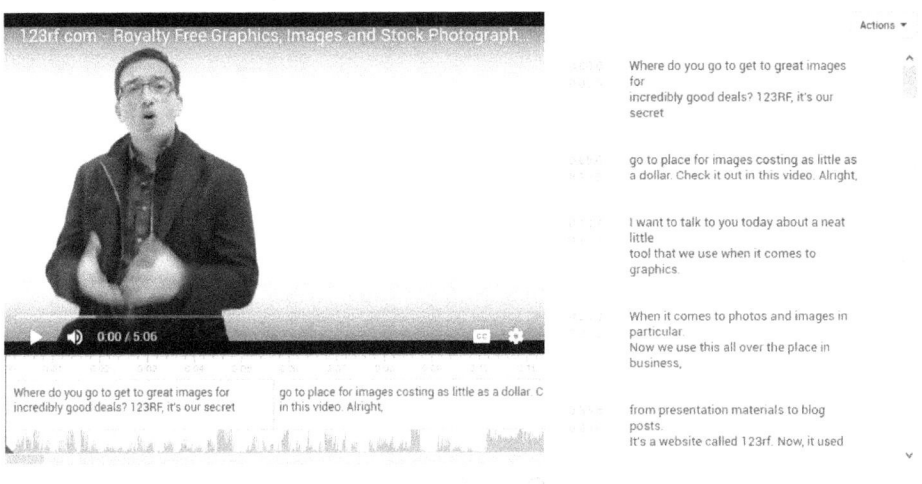

YouTube has now figured out where the transcript matches the video. The subtitles have been published. Now when we go to info and settings, we'll see a posted video in its entirety.

We've got our **thumbnail**, we've got our **title**, **description**, and all of our **tags**. We've now got our **closed caption** in there as well. If you want to double check like I do, go over to the video manager here by clicking on the left.

On the right-hand side, you'll see HD, which means we've uploaded our video in high-definition, beautiful. If you don't have HD video, this little icon will not appear.

You'll see also see a CC icon, which means our closed captions have been logged. If you haven't uploaded your transcript as closed captions, this icon will not appear.

In an ideal world, you want both icons to appear. It's helpful to your YouTube SEO.

Once we know that's been done, we know that video has been fully posted.

We can now move on to the next exciting part, which is measuring the results.

Section Five

Measuring the Results

"LOOK DAVE,

I REALLY DON'T THINK THIS IS

WHAT'S MEANT BY

GETTING MORE HITS"

Section Five / Measuring the Results

The next phase is to see what kind of results we have in the YouTube Algorithm. We can see how that video has ranked even in these early minutes.

Tracking the 123RF Video

It feels good when you have finally got a video up and active on YouTube, but it gets even better as you watch your video climb up through the rankings. Maybe it is on the second or third page right now, depending on the keywords, and depending on how well you did that research back in the preparation period. Watching the video fly up through the ranking from page three to two to one and maybe even through those first ten positions is very exciting.

In the case of the 123RF video, I went in to track the ranking. I don't do these checks in the browser I'm already logged into, because I think that may influence the results, just as it does when hunting for traffic. I close the browser I'm currently in and open a new browser with YouTube where I am not logged in.

Now I go over to my keywords Excel spreadsheet and what we can do is copy and paste the keyword into the search box to see if there are any results.

123rf Keywords
free graphics
low cost graphics
low cost photos
photos you can use
123rf
123rf.com
123rf free
123rf tutorial
royalty free graphics
royalty free images

When you first post the video, it's very early days. Sometimes you get results, sometimes you don't. Sometimes it takes hours for results to show up, maybe even a couple of days, but generally it doesn't take lots of days and that is the great beauty of YouTube.

When I first checked my selected keywords in the new browser, I didn't have any luck. However, things got better when I tried

stock photography tutorial. I scrolled through the results to see if I could see my thumbnail and bam, there it was.

How to Get a White Background in Stock Photography :
Photography Tips & Techniques
by eHow ☑
1 year ago · 2,331 views
Subscribe Now: http://www.youtube.com/subscription_center?add_user=ehow Watch
More: http://www.youtube.com/ehow Getting
HD

Stock Photography Tutorials
by jonesmarc
How to Isolate an Image on White - Photoshop Tutorial [In-Depth]   6 43
How to photograph Shiny Reflective Objects Silver Chrome Met   3 51
View full playlist (3 videos)

123rf.com - Royalty Free Graphics and Images and Stock
Photography - Video Tutorial
by Tim Levy
6 minutes ago · No views
This video about 123rf is for people who need royalty free graphics and royalty free
images. 123rf.com is a web site that offers
NEW   HD

The video was posted six minutes prior and while there were no views just yet, we had gotten an actual result. The video ranked at twenty-eight, great for six minutes. I went over to my spread sheet and said that by six minutes we already have a ranking on **Stock Photography Tutoria**l, at number twenty-eight.

I went back to my browser and right clicked to open a new tab so my browser played the video all the way through. I had the sound turned off so it was not bugging me and I let that video play all the way through so that YouTube knows someone is interested in this and has bothered to watch it in its entirety. This initial video helps get the video ranked.

I know we have got that particular keyword ranking. I looked at the next keyword phrase: **Photography Tips and Tricks**. As I recall we didn't use the phrase **Tips and Tricks** very much and I was now realizing we probably should have. I could go back and change my keywords and titles but that update won't happen immediately. All the same we were ranked for Tips and Tricks and that is great.

stock photography tips and tricks   🔍

Effects Review
by trickphotographyandspecialeffects
1 year ago • 25,044 views
Trick Photography & Special Effects 2nd Edition - Your complete instructional guide on taking breathtaking special effects shots ...

HD

Fotolia Workshop 2012 - Hotel Fotolia - Tips from the trainers (english subtitles)
by fotoliaTV
2 years ago • 4,496 views
In the beginning of June 2012, Europe's leading microstock agency held a workshop that transformed the Hotel Bogota in Berlin ...

HD

123rf com - Royalty Free Graphics and Images and Stock Photography - Video Tutorial
by Tim Levy
8 minutes ago • No views
This video about 123rf is for people who need royalty free graphics and royalty free images. 123rf com is a web site that offers ...

NEW   HD

We ranked at 34 on the second page and the reason we ranked for that was we did use it as a tag. I just didn't use it in those top sentences which I realize now, I should have done.

I expect there is a bit more competition for viewers and there is a wider tail; if you look at the very top of the search results, it says there are 291,000 results. That is a lot of people we are competing with to rank this video. If we go back for example to **Stock Photography Tutorial**, we are going to see it is a lower number: 48,000.

stock photography tips and tricks   Q

Filters ▾   Page 2 of about 49,200 results

I expected I might not rank at all for **Stock Photos** or that it would be further down than page two. **Stock Photography**: I looked at that and found 132,000, so we might have a shot with this one which is fabulous.

As this video matures it will naturally move up the ranking, so you are not stuck forever in one spot.

Within ten minutes this video ranked. The video is listed as **new**. Sometimes it takes a little while for the closed caption to kick in and count towards the rank. I expect the bump from the CC to kick in and lift the ranking in a few hours.

One thing to remember is that the YouTube Algorithm does not update in real time. It takes a couple of hours to update and it usually only updates a couple of times a day. After a couple of hours, I went back to a new YouTube window (one where I was not logged in) and I typed in our keyword search term. On the list we were at number thirty-four, which means the very middle of the second page. When I went to look this time our rank increased to fifteen.

So what was the big difference? **The big difference I believe is the closed caption**. Remember that when we published the video it didn't have closed captions because you didn't have that option but immediately after we published we dropped in the closed caption. Even though it took about two hours, the closed captions had now gone into the search engine algorithm and so suddenly our rank was much higher.

Another search term or keyword we try to rank for was **123RF.** After two hours, we are now in position number four for "123RF" instead of number six. In **123RF Tutorial**, we were in position number three which is already high. For **royalty free graphics** we rose from number eighteen to position nine.

And what about this? I went back to update this manuscript a year after posting, and this video is stable at number 1!

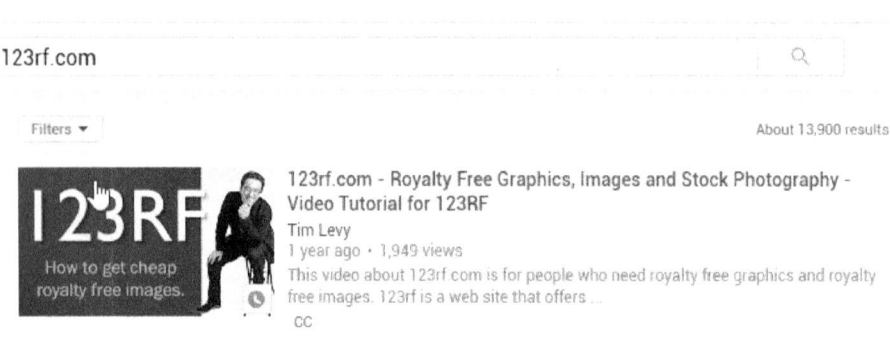

We won't rank high for all the keywords, and sometimes the competition is tough. Still, with ranking in most keywords I anticipate with a few days, as long as the video is good and getting good response, comments and so forth, it will continue to move up the rankings.

Here is a summary of our rankings, having completed the spreadsheet (and updated a year later).

123rf Keywords	6 mins	2 hours	1 year
123rf	34	15	2
123rf.com	15	6	1
123rf free	6	4	1
123rf tutorial	3	3	1
royalty free graphics	18	9	5
royalty free images	-	31	12
stock photography	-	59	-
stock photos	-	-	-
stock photography tips and tricks	34	17	17
stock photography tutorial	28	16	29
stock photography sites	-	39	47

Tracking the VideoHive video

I had a look at the VideoHive video after that. There was nothing for the first keyword. I looked at the second one**: VideoHive Openers** - and there we were on the second page. I tried looking at the word **VideoHive** which I expected to be a fairly high competition keyword and it is. I would be surprised to see anything here.

Remember my little trick here. Right click and open the tab and have this video play without sound so it plays all the way through, indicating to YouTube that it is a successful video.

Here is where we wound up for the Videohive.net video –

VideoHive Keywords	5 minutes	1 year
videohive ✚	-	-
videohive.net	27	2
videohive tutorial	16	4
videohive.net tutorial	3	1
after effects template	-	-
motion graphic templates	29	39
broadcast graphic templates	29	10
videohive after effects template	-	-
videhive templates	-	-
videhive.net templates	3	1
videhive flat design	30	19
videohive after effects	-	-
videohive movie reveals	3	3
videohive movie trailer	27	11
videohive openers	-	-
after effects template tutorial	-	-

Troubleshooting: Fixing or Changing a Keyword

If I do a search for the keyword **videohive.com** that will do me no good because it is a **".net"** site. I can go back into YouTube and fix that keyword.

To do that, I sign back in to YouTube and find my way to the creator's studio once more. I can select the video and go back to the edit info screen. As you can see here the list shows **videohive.com** which is not a real website. I change it to **videohive.net** which is a real website.

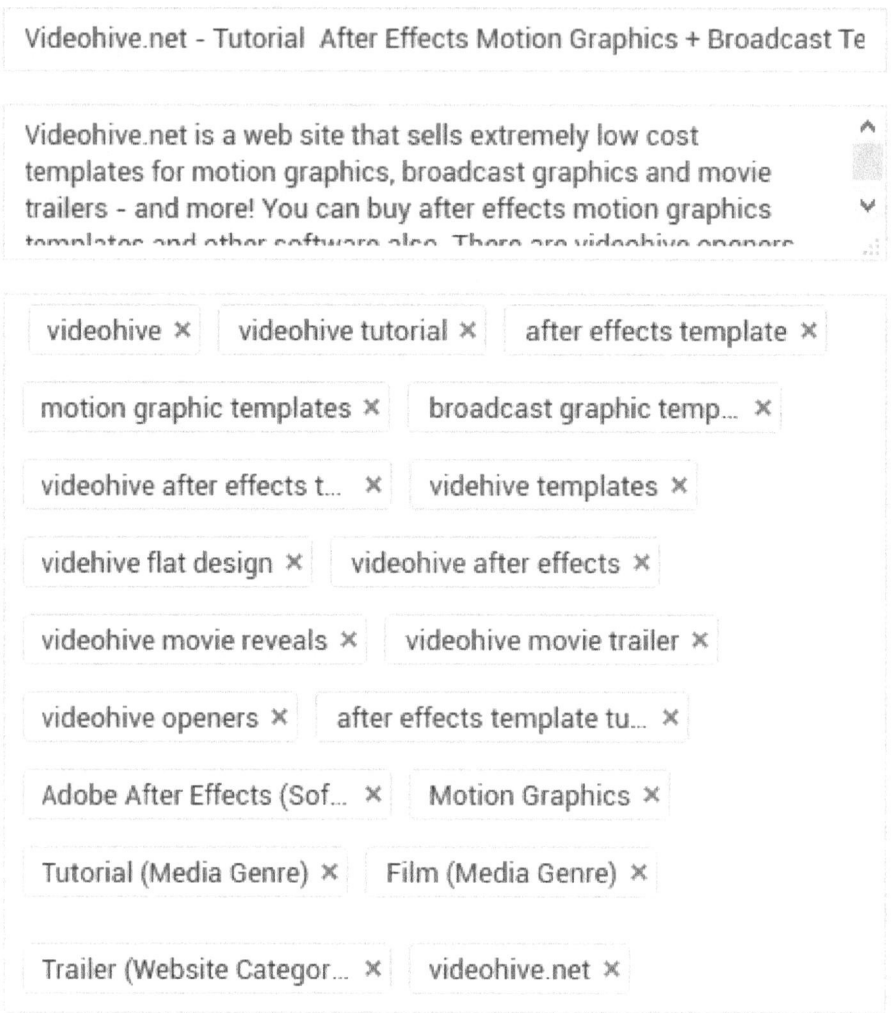

Videohive.net - Tutorial After Effects Motion Graphics + Broadcast Te

Videohive.net is a web site that sells extremely low cost templates for motion graphics, broadcast graphics and movie trailers - and more! You can buy after effects motion graphics templates and other software also. There are videohive openers

| videohive × | videohive tutorial × | after effects template × |

| motion graphic templates × | broadcast graphic temp... × |

| videohive after effects t... × | videhive templates × |

| videhive flat design × | videohive after effects × |

| videohive movie reveals × | videohive movie trailer × |

| videohive openers × | after effects template tu... × |

| Adobe After Effects (Sof... × | Motion Graphics × |

| Tutorial (Media Genre) × | Film (Media Genre) × |

| Trailer (Website Categor... × | videohive.net × |

This fixes our tags and I check to make sure we have already got it correct in the title and in the name. I hit **save changes**.

Remember; just as in original postings, changes might take a while to propagate. Let me show you what I mean: we now know we have one view but if I now search for this again. For a few minutes YouTube will treat this like a new video and will say **no views** even though we know it had one. It will catch up though, and then we should rank better with that corrected keyword.

If I check for keywords such as **After Effects Template** and **Motion Graphics Templates**, I see this video is already ranking. Just as I changed the incorrect **videohive.com** keyword for the corrected **videohive.net** one, we can always add or change keywords to improve hits and ranking. If I search for some combined keywords, I see our video is at number three. You can also help the ranking along by going to a new (unsigned in) YouTube window, right clicking and letting the video play with the sound down.

When I find the video ranking for a keyword or combination of keywords, I right click and let it play itself out again. This shows YouTube the video is successful.

After a few hours, I go in and check again. I start with the **videohive.net** keyword. I find we are now on the front page at position seven; that's up from twenty-seven. **VideoHive tutorial** is now at number nine. These improved results are happening because closed caption is kicking in. **VideoHive Template** is now at number 2 and **flat design** is at sixteen.

You can see this is a dramatic change in a short amount of time, once closed caption kicks in.

Section Six

Wrapping It All Up

"WELL, YOU'VE GONE VIRAL.

THAT'S WHAT YOU WANTED ISN'T IT?"

Section Six / Wrapping It All Up

In YouTube Mastery 101 we looked at the **key concepts** of traffic and SEO.

- What is traffic?
- Why is it important? Why do I care?
- What is YouTube traffic? What is YouTube SEO?

We found out how to manipulate the YouTube algorithm to get the best possible ranking.

- We looked at **video structure**. How do we structure our video to get the most out of YouTube?
- We learned to **prepare the video for posting**, by hunting for keywords, designed a thumbnail, getting a transcript and optimizing our filenames
- We posted the video by **uploading the file**, filing out the **title, tags** and **descriptions**, then **uploaded the thumbnails** and hit the **publish button**
- Then we went back and added the **closed captions**. *Remember, the option to work on this step doesn't become available until after you hit publish.*

- We learned out how to **check the rankings**, and how to adjust the keywords if necessary, and saw how a second push of ratings comes when the closed captions kick in (which might be a couple of hours after they have been uploaded).

- We also learned to give the process a push by signing out and then **searching for our own video** via the keywords, right clicking and letting the video play through with the sound turned down to give the YouTube algorithm the first views to indicate a successful video.

Now, over to you! Create and post some videos, and see your results improve with every try. It is just that easy.

The 10,000 Views

Now at the very beginning of this book, we spoke about building a channel to 10,000 views per month. It's on the front cover, remember?

Well, by now, you've probably done the math for yourself. If you can get a single video to 10,000 views a month, then well done, you. Most likely, however, you'll build a channel of videos all ranking roughly 500-1,500 views per month. Here's a snapshot -

Top 10 Videos

Browse all content

Video	↓ Views	
Fiverr Tutorial - Video on How to U...	3,534	22%
The Google Gamble - Google.com ...	2,297	14%
Digital Marketing Tutorial 2014 - Fr...	1,397	8.7%
Blurb Tutorial - How to Publish A B...	971	6.0%
ThemeForest Tutorial - A Video Tut...	920	5.7%
Facebook- Marketing Tips on How ...	793	4.9%
Fiverr Tips and Tricks Video Tutoria...	770	4.8%
Prezi Presentation Software - How ...	716	4.4%
Producteev Tutorial and Review - H...	612	3.8%
Facebook Boost Post - A Video Tut...	545	3.4%

As you can see, we have some videos up in the multi-thousands and others down at half a thousand. Here's the current total –

Views

16,138 ▼
-4.67% compared to previous period

As you can see, we're down a few points on last month which means we need to add some new videos! Other than that, we're well over 10,000 views. And you can do this too, just get posting, my friends!

The Wild West

Right now, in my opinion, YouTube represents the wild, wild west of the internet. Very few people are utilizing YouTube SEO at all, let alone well. As a result, a minimal effort will achieve an amazing result.

Having said that, it's not going to be like this forever. Eventually, the slow moving giant corporations will figure this out and join the game. And when they do, the space will become more crowded and the game will change.

Much the same thing happened with Google SEO. In the early days when the algorithm was forming, it was possible to get strong results with minimal effort because so few people were playing the game at all. Now, however, the space is crowded and the results have become ... lackluster.

So my advice to you is to jump in quickly! And by all means send us a note through www.timlevyandassociates.com/contact to let us know how you're doing.

Yours on a Friday,

Tim

www.ingramcontent.com/pod-product-compliance
Lightning Source LLC
Chambersburg PA
CBHW070242190526
45169CB00001B/272